Mastering Immutable.js

Better JavaScript development using immutable data

Adam Boduch

BIRMINGHAM - MUMBAI

Mastering Immutable.js

First published: September 2017

Production reference: 1250917

Published by Packt Publishing Ltd.
Livery Place
35 Livery Street
Birmingham
B3 2PB, UK.
ISBN 978-1-78839-511-3

www.packtpub.com

Credits

Author
Adam Boduch

Reviewer
Jurgen Van de Moere

Acquisition Editor
Dominic Shakeshaft

Content Development Editor
Gary Shwartz

Copy Editor
Tom Jacob

Technical Editor
Joel Wilfred D'souza

Project Editor
Suzanne Coutinho

Proofreader
Safis Editing

Production Coordinator
Arvindkumar Gupta

About the Author

Adam Boduch has been involved with large-scale JavaScript development for nearly 10 years. Before moving to the frontend, he worked on several large-scale cloud computing products, using Python and Linux. No stranger to complexity, Adam has practical experience with real-world software systems and the scaling challenges they pose.

He is the author of several JavaScript books, including *React & React Native*, and is passionate about innovative user experiences and high performance.

About the Reviewer

Jurgen Van de Moere is a front-end architect based in Belgium. He began his career in 1999 and worked for more than a decade as a web developer and system engineer for large companies across Europe. In 2012, driven by his passion for Web Technologies, Jurgen decided to specialise in JavaScript and Angular. Since then, he has helped many leading businesses succeed in building secure, maintainable, testable, and scalable Angular applications. In his mission to continually share his knowledge with others, Jurgen serves as a private advisor and mentor to world-renowned businesses and developers around the world.

You won't find Jurgen in the spotlight very often as he loves to spend time with his family, reading books and writing articles. His writings impact thousands of developers a day and are regularly featured by some of the leading publishers in the tech industry.

Jurgen is actively involved in growing the Belgian Angular community as co-organizer of NG-BE, Belgium's first ever Angular conference. In 2016, he was awarded through the Google GDE program as the first ever Google Developer Expert in Belgium for web technologies. You can reach Jurgen at `hire@jvandemo.com`, follow him on Twitter at `https://twitter.com/jvandemo`, or read his articles on `https://jvandemo.com`.

www.PacktPub.com

For support files and downloads related to your book, please visit www.PacktPub.com. Did you know that Packt offers eBook versions of every book published, with PDF and ePub files available? You can upgrade to the eBook version at www.PacktPub.com and as a print book customer, you are entitled to a discount on the eBook copy. Get in touch with us at service@packtpub.com for more details. At www.PacktPub.com, you can also read a collection of free technical articles, sign up for a range of free newsletters and receive exclusive discounts and offers on Packt books and eBooks.

https://www.packtpub.com/mapt

Get the most in-demand software skills with Mapt. Mapt gives you full access to all Packt books and video courses, as well as industry-leading tools to help you plan your personal development and advance your career.

Why subscribe?

- Fully searchable across every book published by Packt
- Copy and paste, print, and bookmark content
- On demand and accessible via a web browser

Customer Feedback

Thanks for purchasing this Packt book. At Packt, quality is at the heart of our editorial process. To help us improve, please leave us an honest review on this book's Amazon page at www.amazon.com/1788395115.

If you'd like to join our team of regular reviewers, you can email us at customerreviews@packtpub.com. We award our regular reviewers with free eBooks and videos in exchange for their valuable feedback. Help us be relentless in improving our products!

Table of Contents

Preface

I like functional programming languages. One of my favorite features is native immutability. Some functional languages, by default, don't let you change values. What's amazing about this capability is that you can't accidentally break your application by mutating data at the wrong time. If you try, the code won't even compile.

I also dislike certain aspects of functional programming languages. On one hand, it's great that immutability is enforced the way it is. On the other hand, there are times when I just need to push aside my functional programming principles and get the job done.

The JavaScript language has many useful functional programming features out of the box. You don't need a library to compose higher-order functions, for example. Something that's difficult to get right with JavaScript is immutability. This is where Immutable.js shines.

When I first heard about Immutable.js, I pictured a library that enforced immutability on JavaScript structures and nothing more. It turns out there's much more. When you're working with immutable structures, you're constantly creating them. The Immutable.js collection API helps you create the structures you need, when you need them.

Since this is a JavaScript library, there's no immutability by default. This allows me to use Immutable.js where immutability matters, and to mutate things when I need to. This is what makes this such an essential library for applications in the real world; pragmatic functional programming that gets the job done.

What this book covers

Chapter 1, *Why Immutable.js?*, explains why you want to use this library.

Chapter 2, *Creating Immutable Data,* helps you get started by creating immutable collections.

Chapter 3, *Persistent Changes,* discusses how to create new data by changing existing data.

Chapter 4, *Filtering Collections and Finding Items,* talks about locating the data that you need.

Chapter 5, *Sequences and Side-Effects,* explains how to iterate over collections in order to use collection data.

Chapter 6, *Sorting Collections,* helps you in get the order right.

Chapter 7, *Mapping and Reducing*, introduces the fundamentals of transforming collection data.

Chapter 8, *Zipping and Flattening*, discusses simplifying iterations and collection structures.

Chapter 9, *Persistent Change Detection*, enables you to determine whether a persistent change method actually changed data.

Chapter 10, *Working with Sets*, explains how to produce unique collection values.

Chapter 11, *Comparing Collections*, talks about figuring out how one collection relates to another.

Chapter 12, *Combining Collections*, helps you build new collections by adding collections together.

Chapter 13, *Declarative Decision Making*, uses immutable collections to help write declarative code.

Chapter 14, *Side-Effects in User Interfaces*, explains rendering UI components with immutable collections.

Chapter 15, *Side-Effects in Node.js*, discusses reading and writing collection data using IO streams.

Chapter 16, *Immutable Architecture*, puts it all together, in the form of a reusable pattern.

What you need for this book

You need a computer, Node.js, and a code editor. Instructions for setting up tools to run the code examples can be found at https://github.com/PacktPublishing/Mastering-Immutablejs.

Who this book is for

This book is for anyone who wants to improve the reliability and performance of their JavaScript code by leveraging the ideas of immutability. Basic JavaScript knowledge is assumed. You should be able to create arrays and objects, manipulate arrays and objects, and create and call functions.

Conventions

In this book, you will find a number of text styles that distinguish between different kinds of information. Here are some examples of these styles and an explanation of their meaning.

Code words in text, database table names, folder names, filenames, file extensions, pathnames, dummy URLs, user input, and Twitter handles are shown as follows: Code words in text are shown as follows: "We can include other contexts through the use of the import statement."

A block of code is set as follows:

```
#import packages into the project
from bs4 import BeautifulSoup
from urllib.request import urlopen
import pandas as pd
```

When we wish to draw your attention to a particular part of a code block, the relevant lines or items are set in bold:

```
import { List } from 'immutable';
const myList = List();
console.log('List', myList instanceof List);
// -> List true
```

New terms and **important words** are shown in bold. Words that you see on the screen, for example, in menus or dialog boxes, appear in the text like this: "In order to download new modules, we will go to **Files | Settings | Project Name | Project Interpreter**."

Warnings or important notes appear like this.

Tips and tricks appear like this.

Reader feedback

Feedback from our readers is always welcome. Let us know what you think about this book—what you liked or disliked. Reader feedback is important for us as it helps us develop titles that you will really get the most out of. To send us general feedback, simply email feedback@packtpub.com, and mention the book's title in the subject of your message. If there is a topic that you have expertise in and you are interested in either writing or contributing to a book, see our author guide at www.packtpub.com/authors.

Customer support

Now that you are the proud owner of a Packt book, we have a number of things to help you to get the most from your purchase.

Downloading the example code

You can download the example code files for this book from your account at http://www.packtpub.com. If you purchased this book elsewhere, you can visit http://www.packtpub.com/support and register to have the files emailed directly to you. You can download the code files by following these steps:

1. Log in or register to our website using your email address and password.
2. Hover the mouse pointer on the **SUPPORT** tab at the top.
3. Click on **Code Downloads & Errata**.
4. Enter the name of the book in the **Search** box.
5. Select the book for which you're looking to download the code files.
6. Choose from the drop-down menu where you purchased this book from.
7. Click on **Code Download**.

Once the file is downloaded, please make sure that you unzip or extract the folder using the latest version of:

- WinRAR / 7-Zip for Windows
- Zipeg / iZip / UnRarX for Mac
- 7-Zip / PeaZip for Linux

The code bundle for the book is also hosted on GitHub at `https://github.com/PacktPublishing/MasteringImmutablejs`. We also have other code bundles from our rich catalog of books and videos available at `https://github.com/PacktPublishing/`. Check them out!

Downloading the color images of this book

We also provide you with a PDF file that has color images of the screenshots/diagrams used in this book. The color images will help you better understand the changes in the output. You can download this file from `https://www.packtpub.com/sites/default/files/downloads/MasteringImmutablejs.pdf`.

Errata

Although we have taken every care to ensure the accuracy of our content, mistakes do happen. If you find a mistake in one of our books—maybe a mistake in the text or the code—we would be grateful if you could report this to us. By doing so, you can save other readers from frustration and help us improve subsequent versions of this book. If you find any errata, please report them by visiting `http://www.packtpub.com/submit-errata`, selecting your book, clicking on the **Errata Submission Form** link, and entering the details of your errata. Once your errata are verified, your submission will be accepted and the errata will be uploaded to our website or added to any list of existing errata under the *Errata* section of that title. To view the previously submitted errata, go to `https://www.packtpub.com/books/content/support` and enter the name of the book in the search field. The required information will appear under the **Errata** section.

Piracy

Piracy of copyrighted material on the internet is an ongoing problem across all media. At Packt, we take the protection of our copyright and licenses very seriously. If you come across any illegal copies of our works in any form on the internet, please provide us with the location address or website name immediately so that we can pursue a remedy. Please contact us at `copyright@packtpub.com` with a link to the suspected pirated material. We appreciate your help in protecting our authors and our ability to bring you valuable content.

Questions

If you have a problem with any aspect of this book, you can contact us at `questions@packtpub.com`, and we will do our best to address the problem.

1
Why Immutable.js?

Immutable.js is yet another JavaScript library. If this makes you cringe, don't worry—I feel your pain. The last thing that JavaScript developers need is another library to learn. Then, I used the library and realized that Immutable.js is one of those gems that you don't have to feel bad about including as a dependency.

This first chapter will show you what Immutable.js is all about. Hopefully, I can dispel any mysteries about Immutable.js while making you want to try it out for yourself.

Here's what you'll learn in this chapter before getting your hands dirty in the chapters that follow:

- Why changes to data are destructive
- What are persistent changes?
- The hybrid functional/object approach used by Immutable.js
- Why data flows in one direction in Immutable.js
- Alternative libraries and approaches to immutability

Mutations are destructive

When you mutate data, you change it. If data is immutable, you can't change it.

 The purpose of Immutable.js is to bring unchangeable data to JavaScript.

Immutability is native to some programming languages. But why is changing data bad, and how does one write software with data that never changes?

Deleting old data

When you first learned how to program, one of the earliest concepts that you were taught was the variable. A **variable** is something that's used to store a value, so of course it's important! When you create a variable and assign its initial value, it feels like you're creating new data. This is because you *are* creating new data.

Then, later on in your code, you assign a new value to your variable. It's a variable, so naturally it *varies*. This might also seem like you're creating new data, which you are; if you assign the value 5 to your variable, then that's a new value that didn't exist before. Here's the catch: you're also destroying data. What if your variable had a value of 2 before you assigned it 5?

This might not seem like a big deal. Isn't a variable supposed to store whatever value you assign to it? Yes, variables work perfectly fine that way. They do exactly what we ask them to do. So, the problem isn't strictly that variables can change their values. Rather, it's a human limitation—we can't reason our way through the huge number of variable changes that happen in our code. This leads to some scary bugs.

A scary class of bugs

Imagine that you're trying to bake a loaf of bread. Nothing fancy, just a plain loaf. You don't even need to look at the recipe—it's just a handful of ingredients, and you've memorized the steps. Now suppose that one or two of your ingredients have been changed without your knowledge. You still follow the steps, and the end result still looks like bread, but then your family eats it. One family member says something tastes off, another doesn't seem to notice anything, while yet another heads straight for the washroom.

These are just some of many possible scenarios that could have played out, and the problems all stemmed from the ingredients used. In other words, because the ingredients were allowed to change, they did change. Consider the game Telephone. In this game, there is a line of people and a message is whispered to the first person in the line. The same message is whispered (allegedly) to the next person, and so on, until the message reaches the last person who then says the message out loud. The ending message is almost never the same as the starting message. Once again, the message changes because it's allowed to change.

When writing software, you're no different from the person making bread using incorrect ingredients or the Telephone game player relaying an incorrect message. The end result is a scary type of bug. If you mess up your bread, can you pinpoint exactly what went wrong? Can you identify the Telephone game players who broke the message? Your variables change because they can. You've written code to make the variables change, and sometimes everything works exactly as you want it to. But when something goes wrong, it's very difficult to figure out what went wrong.

Persisting changes

If data isn't supposed to change, just how are we supposed to get anything done? How do we move the state of an application along from one state to the next if our data is immutable? The answer is that every operation that you perform on immutable data creates new immutable data. These are called **persistent changes**, because the original data is persisted. The new data that's created as a result of running the operation contains the changes. When we call an operation on this new data, it returns new data, and so on.

What are we supposed to do with the old data when we make a persistent change that results in new data? The answer is – it depends. Sometimes, you'll just replace the old data with the new data. Yes, the variable is changed, but it's replaced with an entirely new reference. This means that something that is still referencing the old data is never affected by your persistent changes.

The Immutable.js approach

Different JavaScript libraries each have their own approach to deal with certain things. For example, React relies on JSX—an XML dialect embedded in JavaScript for declaring user interface components. Lodash exposes lots of little functions, some of which can be chained together to simplify complex code. The idea behind Immutable.js is to expose a small number of collection classes as its API. How does it work?

A collections API

A **collection** in JavaScript refers to anything that can be iterated over, for example, when using a `for..of` loop. In practice, this means arrays and objects. Arrays and objects are collections of values; the only difference between them is how you look up values. An **array** is an indexed collection, because you use a numerical index to lookup a value. An **object** is a keyed collection, because you use a key string to lookup a value.

The issue with these primitive JavaScript collection types is that they can change; that is, they're not immutable. The collections exposed by Immutable.js feel a lot like native arrays and objects. In fact, you can take an array or an object and use it to construct an Immutable.js collection. You can also turn an Immutable.js collection into a JavaScript array or object.

This is the extent of the Immutable.js API. You use collection classes to hold your immutable data. To use this immutable data, you call methods on these collections, which is at the very heart of the Immutable.js API.

Collection methods return new data

Let's say that you have an Immutable.js collection: `coll1`. Then, you call a method to insert a new value into the collection: `push('newValue')`. This is what a persistent change looks like: `coll1` persists and `push()` returns a new collection that includes the new value.

Not all collection methods are mutative. For example, if you want to filter a collection so that only items that pass a given criteria are returned, you would call the `filter()` method. This would result in a new collection, just like adding a new item would result in a new collection. The difference is that `filter()` isn't a persistent change—it's part of a **sequence transformation**.

Think of a sequence transformation as an Instagram filter. You have the original collection: the picture. Then, you have a `filter()` transformation, which takes the original picture data and rearranges some of the pixel data. You want to be able to see the results of the filter, but you don't want to change the original. The filter is just a view of the original.

Chaining method calls

Immutable data doesn't just sit inside of a constant. Somehow, your applications need to make use of this data. These are called side-effects. A **side-effect** is something that is effected by immutable data, such as rendering data on the screen in a user interface or writing data to a file. By contrast, operations performed on immutable collections are either persistent changes or sequence transformations, both of which result in new collections. These operations don't have any side-effects; they just result in new data being created. Another term used for functions that don't cause side-effects is **pure functions**.

With Immutable.js, you start with a collection of immutable data and work your way toward some sort of side-effect. In functional programming, it's generally best to avoid side-effects due to the problems they cause. But side-effects are unavoidable. Without them, your software cannot interact with its environment. By chaining together Immutable.js collection methods, you can write clean and concise code that transforms immutable data into something that you need—something that a side-effect can use.

Unidirectional data flow

React and Flux have popularized the concept of unidirectional data flow as the fundamental concept that drives web application architecture. A **unidirectional data flow** is exactly what it sounds like—data that flows in one direction. It's a simple idea, but it's an important mindset to adopt when thinking about immutable data.

What other direction is there?

The best way to visualize unidirectional data flow is in a top-down fashion. Data starts in one state at the top, changes state as it flows downward, ending with a side-effect that does something with the data. When this is enforced as a property of the architecture, side-effects are predictable. We can easily trace the starting point of data, through the transformations it makes, ending with the visible side-effect.

When we don't enforce a unidirectional data flow, it's difficult to trace cause and effect. This is the main reason that Facebook started promoting the concept with the creation of Flux—to prevent components from changing state at will and passing the changed state on to another component. For example, let's say that you aren't using immutable data, and that one component changes its state in response to an event. Then some other component that references this state renders itself, causing its state to change as a result of the first change. These are nothing more than uncontrolled side-effects.

Immutable.js is a low-level library compared to the ideas of Flux or a UI component library such as React. Even if you're not using either of these, you can still leverage Immutable.js to build a unidirectional architecture.

Subscriptions are out

One approach to handling data that changes is to **observe** it. This means using some mechanism to attach a listener callback function that's called whenever the data changes. For example, you could have data that models a user interface component, and when that data changes, you would render the component so that it reflects the changed data.

To set up subscriptions like this will require data that can change, which we don't want. Since we're working with immutable data that never changes, subscriptions are a dead end. This means that you have to rethink your approach for notifying components about the state of your data. The rule of thumb with immutable architectures is that only new data is passed around when things change.

Data is only created

Let's revisit the visualization of data flowing from top to bottom, ending with a side-effect. Along the way, we're either changing the state of data with persistent changes, or we're shaping the data that we need using sequence transformations. From the beginning to the end of this flow, we're only creating new data.

The chained Immutable.js collection method calls result in new data—every time. This means that if we make a mistake and accidentally try to use data in a way that falls outside of the unidirectional flow that we're following, Immutable.js will protect us from ourselves. When this happens, the result is often a broken application that doesn't work. This is better than a half-working application that has mutability bugs hidden deep inside of it.

For example, suppose that we call set() on an immutable map to set a value, expecting that simply calling this method would be enough to change the state of the map. But since the set() method is a persistent change, it doesn't change the map—it creates and returns a new map. So while we weren't expecting this behavior, it's better than accidentally changing the state of something.

Implicit side-effects are hard to do

Side-effects in code that uses mutable data are **implicit**. Immutable.js, on the other hand, promotes **explicit** side-effects by placing them at the end of a method call chain. This makes the side-effects in your code easy to spot, and easy to reason our way through the sequence of transformations and persistent changes that lead up to the side-effect occurring.

Implicit side-effects are problematic because we don't have any meaningful way to track them. For example, you change some data that results in four function calls being made. Do any of them have side-effects? Two of them? All of them? Do the side-effects cascade into other side-effects? We're creating too much work for our brains to handle here.

The trick with Immutable.js is to make explicit the things that matter when you're reading code. This means quickly figuring out what caused a given side-effect to occur. On the other hand, you can't make everything explicit otherwise you'd have a mountain of code to sift through. The implicitness of Immutable.js comes with piecing together data by gluing it together using chaining—there's a lot going on behind the scenes that you don't need to think about.

Other libraries similar to Immutable.js

Immutable.js isn't the only library out there that does what it does. While it is unique in its approach to handling immutable data, it's never a bad idea to compare one library with another. What, exactly, are we comparing it with, though?

What are we comparing?

There's no point in comparing a library such as Immutable.js with something that has no notion of functional programming or immutability. For instance, Angular is a framework for building applications, and observing changes in state is a core pattern. This is something that Immutable.js doesn't do. Comparing Immutable.js with something such as React doesn't make much sense either. Despite the fact that React honors concepts such as avoiding side-effects, we wouldn't be comparing apples with apples, as they do different things at different levels of abstraction.

Some criteria that you would use to compare Immutable.js with other libraries include the following:

- Is it a low-level library?
- Does it support the notion of immutability?
- Does it have the concept of collections?
- How large is the API compared with that of Immutable.js?
- How efficiently can it handle immutable data?

Lodash is a good bet

Lodash is a popular utility library that does a lot of the same things as Immutable.js. It supports the notion of immutability and avoids side-effects. It also supports the concept of collections. Its approach to efficiency is different from what Immutable.js does, but it's there. It might have a larger API than Immutable.js, but it's not that much larger.

The two libraries differ greatly in their overall approach and design, but they're comparable in the aspects that matter. Learning Lodash before switching to Immutable.js isn't a total loss and vice versa. You won't know which libraries work best for you until you write code that uses them.

We'll start writing Immutable.js code in a moment.

Summary

This chapter introduced you to the conceptual foundation of Immutable.js. Immutable data is how we prevent unwanted side-effects. With Immutable.js collections, everything results in new data. This includes changing the collection somehow—these are called persistent changes. It also includes shaping the data in order to do something with it—these are called sequence transformations.

The typical Immutable.js pattern involves chaining collection method calls together—the persistent changes and sequence transformations—ending with a side-effect.

In the next chapter, we'll write some code that creates Immutable.js collections.

2
Creating Immutable Data

The starting point of writing any Immutable.js code is to create an immutable collection. In this chapter, that's just what we'll do. There are a number of ways to create immutable collections, and you'll learn what they are and when they are appropriate to use. Specifically, we'll look at the following:

- Using Immutable.js constructors
- Using utility functions to create collections
- Parsing JavaScript types into Immutable.js collections

Immutable.js constructors

The Immutable.js API exposes immutable collections as classes. You then use these classes to create new collection instances. This is just like any other object-oriented JavaScript API that exposes classes. There is one important difference, though—these aren't real classes.

There are a number of internal implementation reasons for why Immutable.js doesn't expose actual classes as its API. One reason is that in some cases, collection instances can be reused, such as when creating empty collections. The only thing to keep in mind is that you never need to use the new keyword when creating Immutable.js data.

The types of Immutable.js data

The entirety of the Immutable.js API is represented by the following types:

- Lists
- Maps

- Ordered maps
- Sets
- Ordered sets
- Sequences
- Stacks
- Records

Of these types, we'll only use a few consistently throughout the applications in this book. Each type has it's own operations exposed as methods, and you can easily change from one collection type to another. Of course, it would help if you knew what these types are, so let's start there.

Lists

A **list** is like a JavaScript array. It's an **indexed collection**, meaning that the same type of indexes that you would use with an array will also work with lists. The notation is different, though—you use methods to get and set data instead of the [ ] notation, as shown here:

```
import { List } from 'immutable';
const myList = List();
console.log('List', myList instanceof List);
// -> List true
```

Maps

A **map** is like a JavaScript object. It's a **keyed collection**, meaning that the same types of keys that you would use with JavaScript objects also work with maps. Immutable.js maps are also like native JavaScript Map instances in that they can use anything as a key—not just strings:

```
import { Map } from 'immutable';
const myMap = Map();
console.log('Map', myMap instanceof Map);
// -> Map true
```

Ordered maps

An **ordered map** is just like a map except that the order in which items are added is preserved. This type of map behaves like a list, only instead of looking up values using numerical indexes, you can use any key you like:

```
import { OrderedMap } from 'immutable';
const myOrderedMap = OrderedMap();
console.log('OrderedMap', myOrderedMap instanceof OrderedMap);
// -> OrderedMap true
```

Sets

A **set** is like a list in that it's an indexed collection. There are two things about sets that are different from lists. First, sets can only hold unique values—duplicates are silently ignored. Second, the iteration order of sets isn't defined. This means that the index of a given value doesn't necessarily reflect the iteration order of the value:

```
import { Set } from 'immutable';
const mySet = Set();
console.log('Set', mySet instanceof Set);
// -> Set true
```

Ordered sets

An **ordered set** is just like a set. It doesn't allow duplicate values, but it does maintain the iteration order. This works the same way as with an ordered map—the iteration order is the same as the insertion order:

```
import { OrderedSet } from 'immutable';
const myOrderedSet = OrderedSet();
console.log('OrderedSet', myOrderedSet instanceof OrderedSet);
// -> OrderedSet true
```

Sequences

A **sequence** is one or more operations that lazily evaluate items from a collection. Sequences often start off as another type of collection, such as a list or map. You convert collections into sequences when you want to perform some sort of transformation, like this:

```
import { Seq } from 'immutable';
const mySeq = Seq();
console.log('Seq', mySeq instanceof Seq);
// -> Seq true
```

Stacks

A **stack** is like a list because it's an indexed collection. The main difference with stacks is that they're really good at adding and removing values from the front of the collection. If you're implementing something that's **first-in, first-out** (**FIFO**), stacks are a good bet. Otherwise, stay away from stacks:

```
import { Stack } from 'immutable';
const myStack = Stack();
console.log('Stack', myStack instanceof Stack);
// -> Stack true
```

Records

A **record** is closer to a JavaScript object than to an Immutable.js map. The idea here is that records have a predetermined set of allowable string keys, which can specify default values when not provided:

```
const MyRecord = Record({});
const myRecord = new MyRecord();
console.log('Record', myRecord instanceof Record);
// -> Record true
```

Passing JavaScript collections

You can pass native JavaScript collections, such as objects and arrays, to Immutable.js collections, such as maps and lists. This is one way to provide immutable collections with initial values. For example, you can pass the list constructor an array, as follows:

```
const myList = List([1, 2, 3]);
console.log('myList', myList.get(1));
// -> myList 2
```

The `Map` constructors work the same way, except you pass it an object:

```
const myMap = Map({ a: 1, b: 2, c: 3 });
console.log('myMap', myMap.get('b'));
// -> myMap 2
```

Passing array or object literals to Immutable.js collections like this is fine. You should avoid passing in references to arrays or objects, however. The reason is that once you create an Immutable.js collection, the data is supposed to be immutable. If you have a reference to a mutable array or object in your code, this just leads to confusion.

Passing Immutable.js collections

Another scenario for passing data to Immutable.js constructors is for passing other Immutable.js collections. For example, let's say that you have a map instance, just like the one that we created in the preceding section. You can then do the following:

```
const firstMap = Map({ a: 1, b: 2, c: 3 });
console.log('myMap', myMap.get('a'));
// -> myMap 1
```

As expected, you get a new map instance in the `firstMap` constant. Now let's use this first instance as the input for creating another map:

```
const myMap = Map(firstMap);
console.log('firstMap === myMap', firstMap === myMap);
// -> firstMap === myMap true
```

Wait, if Immutable.js maps are immutable, how can `firstMap` be the same reference as `myMap`? This is a trick that Immutable.js uses to avoid having to create another instance of the exact same collection. By doing this, you're not actually violating any kind of immutability constraints. The collection that is passed to `Map()` can't change, so creating a copy of it is wasteful.

This can be useful if you're creating a function that accepts a collection as an argument:

```
const myFunc = map => Map(map).toJS();

console.log('myFunc(object)', myFunc({ a: 1, b: 2, c: 3 }));
// -> myFunc(object) { a: 1, b: 2, c: 3 }
console.log('myFunc(map)', myFunc(myMap));
// -> myFunc(map) { a: 1, b: 2, c: 3 }
```

Rule of thumb: it's never a bad idea to wrap a collection in a collection constructor so that you get consistent results.

Using the of() method

Collection types in Immutable.js have a static `of()` method. This method is an alternative to using the collection constructor. The one downside to using the constructor approach is that you have to pass in a JavaScript literal. You have to build and allocate memory for a structure that you're not actually using.

The `of()` method uses the arguments that are passed to it as the collection items.

Lists of values

You can use the `of()` method to create lists of values as follows:

```
const myList = List.of(1, 2, 3);
console.log('myList', myList.toJS());
// -> myList [ 1, 2, 3 ]
```

Maps of values

You can use the `of()` method to create key-value maps:

```
const myMap = Map.of(
  'a', 1,
  'b', 2,
  'c', 3
);
console.log('myMap', myMap.toJS());
// -> myMap { a: 1, b: 2, c: 3 }
```

The trick here is to alternate between the key and value arguments that are passed to `of()`.

Sets of values

You can use the `of()` method to create sets of values, as shown here:

```
const mySet = Set.of(1, 2, 3);
console.log('mySet', mySet.toJS());
// -> mySet [ 1, 2, 3 ]
```

Sequences of values

You can use the `of()` method to create value sequences, as follows:

```
const mySeq = Seq.of(1, 2, 3);
console.log('mySeq', mySeq.toJS());
// -> mySeq [ 1, 2, 3 ]
```

Parsing data using the fromJS() function

Immutable.js has one more tool for creating immutable data in addition to everything we've looked at so far in this chapter. The `fromJS()` function is similar to a JSON parser, because it parses the same types of JavaScript objects that you'll see when you parse JSON strings: objects and arrays.

Parsing JavaScript arrays

You can parse a regular JavaScript array, resulting in a list, as shown here:

```
import { fromJS } from 'immutable';
const myList = fromJS([1, 2, 3]);
console.log('myList', myList.get(0));
// -> myList 1
```

This is just like passing the array to the `List` constructor.

Parsing JavaScript objects

You can parse a regular JavaScript object, resulting in a map:

```
const myMap = fromJS({
  one: 1,
  two: 2,
  three: 3
});
console.log('myMap', myMap.get('one'));
// -> myMap 1
```

Once again, this is just like passing the object literal to the Map constructor.

Parsing complex structures

The real power of the fromJS() function is its ability to turn complex JavaScript objects into complex immutable collections:

```
const myMap = fromJS({
  a: {
    b: ['c', 'd'],
    e: {
      f: 'g',
      h: 'i'
    }
  }
});
console.log(
  'myMap nested list',
  myMap.getIn(['a', 'b']).toJS()
);
// -> myMap nested list [ 'c', 'd' ]

console.log('myMap nested value', myMap.getIn(['a', 'b', 1]));
// -> myMap nested value d
```

The fromJS() function will recursively transform native JavaScript structures into their immutable counterparts; this means for both lists and maps. One use case for this function is when the initial data that your application uses is based on JSON data, and you need a way to translate it into Immutable.js collections. Without fromJS(), this would be deceptively difficult.

Summary

In this chapter, you were introduced to the various types of collections found in Immutable.js. We then looked at some code that creates new instances of these collections. Most of the time, you'll want to pass some initial data to a collection when it's created. There are a number of ways to create collections with initial data, including passing native JavaScript types to the constructors and using the `of()` static method. We then looked at the `fromJS()` function for when you need to parse complex JavaScript structures into their Immutable.js counterparts.

In the next chapter, you'll learn how to mutate your collections using persistent change methods.

3
Persistent Changes

Immutable data cannot change. The state of your applications must change, however, otherwise they would be completely static. To cope with changing the application state, Immutable.js collections use **persistent changes**. A persistent change involves first copying the target collection and then making the change in the copy.

The focus of this chapter is on some of the collection methods that implement persistent changes. You'll learn about the following:

- Adding values to collections
- Setting and updating collection values
- Removing values from collections
- Emptying collections
- Tracking the change history of collections

Adding values to collections

The two main collection types on which we'll call persistent change methods are lists and maps. When you call a method to add a new value to a collection, you have to store the result somewhere because persistent changes only create data; they never destroy data.

Pushing values to lists

You can push a new value onto a list using the `push()` method, as follows:

```
const myList = List.of(1, 2, 3);
const myChangedList = myList.push(4);

console.log('myList', myList.toJS());
// -> myList [ 1, 2, 3 ]
console.log('myChangedList', myChangedList.toJS());
// -> myChangedList [ 1, 2, 3, 4 ]
```

The end result of calling `push(4)` is a new list. If you want to make use of this list, you have to store it somewhere. In this example, we just want to print the JSON representation of the list, and as you can see, 4 is added to `myChangedList`. You can also see that the contents of `myList` haven't changed. Of course not—it's immutable!

Adding key-value pairs to maps

With maps, we use the `set()` method to add new values. Like the `push()` method used with lists, `set()` results in a new map:

```
const myMap = Map.of(
  'one', 1,
  'two', 2,
  'three', 3
);
const myChangedMap = myMap.set('four', 4);

console.log('myMap', myMap.toJS());
// -> myMap { one: 1, two: 2, three: 3 }
console.log('myChangedMap', myChangedMap.toJS());
// -> myChangedMap { one: 1, two: 2, three: 3, four: 4 }
```

You have to supply the new key for the map, which can be any type of value, not just strings, along with the value itself. This results in the new map being stored in `myChangedMap`, which has the key-value pair that you've just set.

Chaining value insertion methods

When you need to insert more than one value into a collection, you have to call push() or set() multiple times. Instead of storing the new collection every time that you call the method, you can chain the method calls together. You can store the result of this chained call, which is the last collection. The other collections are called **intermediary collections**, which are freed the next time the garbage collector runs.

 Immutable.js can copy collections efficiently because it only copies the parts of the collection that it absolutely needs to copy. When you make persistent changes, most of the old collection data is shared with the new collection. It can do this because most of the collection data hasn't changed, so it would be wasteful just to throw it to the garbage collector.

Pushing multiple list values

Now let's try pushing multiple values to a list:

```
const myList = List.of(1, 2, 3);
const myChangedList = myList
  .push(4)
  .push(5, 6)
  .push(7, 8)
  .push(9);

console.log('myList', myList.toJS());
// -> myList [ 1, 2, 3 ]
console.log('myChangedList', myChangedList);
// -> myChangedList List [ 1, 2, 3, 4, 5, 6, 7, 8, 9 ]
```

Here, the first three calls to push() create intermediary lists—you don't actually use them for anything other than as steps for building a new list. The final call to push() produces the value that ends up in myChangedList. You can see that push() accepts multiple values to add to the list. Of course, it would be better to make one call instead of four where possible. However, this isn't always possible depending on how your code is organized. I'm also using this as an opportunity to illustrate a concept.

Adding multiple map key-value pairs

You can follow the same approach with maps when you need to add more than one value at the same time. Instead of chaining together the `push()` calls as you would with a list, you call `set()`:

```
const myMap = Map.of(
  'one', 1,
  'two', 2,
  'three', 3
);
const myChangedMap = myMap
  .set('four', 4)
  .set('five', 5)
  .set('six', 6);

console.log('myMap', myMap.toJS());
// -> myMap { one: 1, two: 2, three: 3 }
console.log('myChangedMap', myChangedMap.toJS());
// -> myChangedMap { one: 1, two: 2,
// ->                three: 3, four: 4,
// ->                five: 5, six: 6 }
```

The first two calls to `set()` create intermediary maps, while the last call to `set()` produces the final map that ends up in `myChangedMap`.

The `set()` method is used to set new map values and to update existing map values. This poses a problem if you don't want to set a map value for a key that already exists. You can check if a given key already exists in your map using the `has()` method.

Changing collection values

Once you've added data to your collection, you'll probably need to change it. Lists and maps each have two approaches to change existing values.

Changing list values

Lists can either set a value or update a value. The distinction is subtle, so let's compare the two approaches now.

Setting list values

When you set list values using the `set()` method, you're changing an existing value. More specifically, you're overwriting the current value at a given index with a new value:

```
const myList = List.of(1);
const myChangedList = myList.set(0, 2);

console.log('myList', myList.toJS());
// -> myList [ 1 ]
console.log('myChangedList', myChangedList.toJS());
// -> myChangedList [ 2 ]
```

You're updating the first list value—because the index you're passing to `set()` is 0—with a value of 2. Using `set()` like this is a good choice when you know ahead of time what the new value should be. But what about when the new value depends on the current value?

Updating list values

When the new value of a list item depends on the current value, you can use the `update()` method instead of `set()`. It takes a function that gets the current value as an argument and the return value is used as the new value, as shown here:

```
const myList = List.of(
  Map.of('total', 0, 'step', 5),
  Map.of('total', 5, 'step', 10)
);

const increment = map => map.set(
  'total',
  map.get('total') + map.get('step')
);

const myChangedList = myList
  .update(0, increment)
  .update(1, increment);

console.log('myList', myList.toJS());
// -> myList [ { total: 0, step: 5 }, { total: 5, step: 10 } ]
console.log('myChangedList', myChangedList.toJS());
// -> myChangedList [ { total: 5, step: 5 }, { total: 15, step: 10 } ]
```

Each value in this list is a map with two keys: total and step. The increment() function updates the total value based on its current value and the step value. The function then returns the new map that's created by calling set(). If you know the index of the list value that you want to update, you can pass the increment() function to update(), along with the index. In this example, I've updated both list items.

We could have achieved the same result by calling set() on the list, but this would involve manually getting the value from the list first, since we depend on it. Using update() is simpler because the value that we need is given to us as a function argument.

Changing map values

Map values are changed in a similar way as lists. In fact, you use the same two methods: set() and update().

Setting map values

The set() method for maps is used to add and to change collection values. If the key that's being set doesn't exist, then the key-value pair is set for the first time. If the key does exist, then the previous value of that key is replaced with the new value, as follows:

```
const myMap = Map.of('one', 1);
const myChangedMap = myMap.set('one', 'one');

console.log('myMap', myMap.toJS());
// -> myMap { one: 1 }
console.log('myChangedMap', myChangedMap.toJS());
// -> myChangedMap { one: 'one' }
```

Calling set() produces a new map, because all Immutable.js mutations are persistent changes.

Updating map values

Let's revisit the earlier example where we called `update()` on a list. Inside of the update function, `increment()`, we used `set()` to change the value of map. Map was the list value that we were updating. Let's make `map` use the `update()` method as well:

```
const increment = map => map.update(
  'total',
  t => t + map.get('step')
);
```

Instead of having to call `map.get('total')`, `total` is passed in as the function argument.

Chaining collection mutation methods

You've seen how you can chain collection insertion methods together and that there are two types of collection mutation method. Since each of these methods is a persistent change, they return a new collection, which means that you can chain together complex mutation behavior:

```
const myList = List.of(1, 2, 3);
const myMap = Map.of('one', 1, 'two', 2);

const myChangedList = myList
  .push(4)
  .set(3, 5)
  .update(3, n => n + 5);

const myChangedMap = myMap
  .set('three', 3)
  .set('three', 5)
  .update('three', t => t + 5);

console.log('myList', myList.toJS());
// -> myList [ 1, 2, 3 ]
console.log('myMap', myMap.toJS());
// -> myMap { one: 1, two: 2 }
console.log('myChangedList', myChangedList.toJS());
// -> myChangedList [ 1, 2, 3, 10 ]
console.log('myChangedMap', myChangedMap.toJS());
// -> myChangedMap { one: 1, two: 2, three: 10 }
```

Here, we're mutating a list and a map by chaining together insertion methods and mutation methods. A key design trait of the Immutable.js API is that the list methods and the map methods are the same. The obvious difference is push() versus set() for inserting items into lists and maps.

Removing values from collections

Another type of persistent change that you'll want to make is to remove values from collections. Both lists and maps have methods to remove values from them, which results in new collections.

Removing values from lists

If you know the index of the list value that you want to remove, you can pass the index to the remove() method to create a new list without the removed value, as follows:

```
const myList = List.of(1, 2, 3);
const myChangedList = myList.remove(0);

console.log('myList', myList.toJS());
// -> myList [ 1, 2, 3 ]
console.log('myChangedList', myChangedList.toJS());
// -> myChangedList [ 2, 3 ]
```

You can see here that myChangedList results from calling remove(0). It's a new list, without the first value.

Removing values from maps

Maps have a remove() method that works the same way as the list version. The only difference is that it takes a key as the argument instead of an index:

```
const myMap = Map.of(
  'one', 1,
  'two', 2,
  'three', 3
);
const myChangedMap = myMap.remove('one');

console.log('myMap', myMap.toJS());
// -> myMap { one: 1, two: 2, three: 3 }
```

```
console.log('myChangedMap', myChangedMap.toJS());
// -> myChangedMap { three: 3, two: 2 }
```

By calling remove('one') on myMap, you get myChangedMap, a new map without the removed key.

Chaining collection removal methods

If you have more than one value to remove from a collection, you can chain together removal method calls, as follows:

```
const myList = List.of(1, 2, 3, 4);
const myMap = Map.of(
  'one', 1, 'two', 2,
  'three', 3, 'four', 4,
  'five', 5, 'six', 6
);

const myChangedList = myList
  .remove(1)
  .remove(1);

const myChangedMap = myMap
  .remove('six')
  .removeAll(['five', 'four', 'three']);

console.log('myList', myList.toJS());
// -> myList [ 1, 2, 3, 4 ]
console.log('myMap', myMap.toJS());
// -> myMap { one: 1, two: 2, three: 3, four: 4, five: 5, six: 6 }
console.log('myChangedList', myChangedList.toJS());
// -> myChangedList [ 1, 4 ]
console.log('myChangedMap', myChangedMap.toJS());
// -> myChangedMap { one: 1, two: 2 }
```

There are two identical removal calls to the list—remove(1). What's up with that? Chaining removal calls to remove list items can be tricky because removing one value causes every value to the right of it to change its index. At first, the index 1 points to the value 2. Once it's removed, the index 1 points to the value 3.

With maps, you have a couple of options for removing more than one key-value pair. You can chain together calls to remove(), or you can pass multiple keys to the removeAll() method.

Emptying collections

Sometimes, you need to empty your collections. For example, if the user navigates to a different part of the application, you could be left with collection data that you no longer need. Instead of deleting the collection reference, you could just empty it.

Replacing collections with new instances

The simplest way to empty a collection is to replace it with a new instance, as shown here:

```
const empty = (collection) => {
  if (collection instanceof List) {
    return List();
  }
  if (collection instanceof Map) {
    return Map();
  }
  return null;
};

const myList = List.of(1, 2);
const myMap = Map.of('one', 1, 'two', 2);

const myEmptyList = empty(myList);
const myEmptyMap = empty(myMap);

console.log('myList', myList.toJS());
// -> myList [ 1, 2 ]
console.log('myEmptyList', myEmptyList.toJS());
// -> myEmptyList []
console.log('myMap', myMap.toJS());
// -> myMap { one: 1, two: 2 }
console.log('myEmptyMap', myEmptyMap.toJS());
// -> myEmptyMap {}
```

We've created a little helper function called `empty()`. The idea is that it accepts either a list or map as its argument. Depending on the type of collection, a new instance is returned. Then, we can assign this new value to `myEmptyList`. Remember, as long as `myList` is referenced, it will never be garbage-collected. If you don't want this to happen, you could store the collection in a variable instead of in a constant. Then, `empty()` can simply replace the old collection:

```
var myList = List.of(1, 2);
myList = empty(myList);
```

Now, the garbage collector can pick up the first collection with the values 1 and 2.

Using the clear() method

You don't actually have to create a utility function to empty collections by replacing them with new instances. The clear() method does the same thing:

```
const myList = List.of(1, 2);
const myMap = Map.of('one', 1, 'two', 2);

// Create new instances by emptying the
// existing instances.
const myEmptyList = myList.clear();
const myEmptyMap = myMap.clear();

console.log('myList', myList.toJS());
// -> myList [ 1, 2 ]
console.log('myEmptyList', myEmptyList.toJS());
// -> myEmptyList []
console.log('myMap', myMap.toJS());
// -> myMap { one: 1, two: 2 }
console.log('myEmptyMap', myEmptyMap.toJS());
// -> myEmptyMap {}
```

The benefit with the clear() method is that you don't have to invent a utility function that returns new collection instances based on type. Another advantage is that the clear() method will first check to see if the collection is already empty and, if so, it will return the current collection.

 Immutable.js does something neat when it creates new collections. The first time an empty collection is created, let's say a list, that same list instance is reused whenever an empty list is needed. If you create an empty list (List()), or clear a list (myList.clear()), the same instance is reused every time. This is only possible because collections are immutable.

Keeping track of changes

With persistent changes, you leave behind a trail of breadcrumbs that lets you time travel back to any point in your data's past. Whether or not you choose to keep track of these changes is entirely up to you. The need to do this depends on what you're building. For example, it might be useful to be able to roll back changes made to immutable data collections.

Let's implement an abstraction that wraps an Immutable.js collection, augmenting it with history tracking capabilities:

```
import { List, Stack } from 'immutable';

// Names of List and Map methods that perform
// persistent changes. These are the methods that
// we want to build history from.
const persistentChanges = [
  'set',
  'delete',
  'deleteAll',
  'clear',
  'update',
  'merge',
  ...
];

// Where the history for a given collection is stored.
const mutations = new WeakMap();

// Defines proxy behavior for collection instances.
// It's a way to trap method calls and redirect them
// to instances in the mutations map.
const historyHandler = {
  get(target, key) {
    // Before we do anything, make sure that the
    // target collection has a Stack instance in
    // the mutations map.
    if (!mutations.has(target)) {
      mutations.set(
        target,
        Stack().unshift(target)
      );
    }

    // Get the mutation history for this collection.
    const stack = mutations.get(target);

    // Check if the caller is calling one of the
    // recognized persistent change methods.
    if (persistentChanges.includes(key)) {
      // Return a function that calls the method in question
      // on the most recent stack item.
      return (...args) => {
        const result = stack.first()[key](...args);

        // Store the result as the newest item on the stack.
```

```
        mutations.set(
          target,
          stack.unshift(result)
        );

        // Return the result like normal.
        return result;
      };

    // The caller is calling the undo() method. Remove the
    // first item on the stack, if there's more than
    // one item.
    } else if (key === 'undo') {
      return () =>
        mutations.set(
          target,
          stack.count() > 1 ? stack.shift() : stack
        );
    }
    // Not a persistent change method, just call it and
    // return the result.
    return stack.first()[key];
  }
};

// Wraps a List instance with the historyHandler proxy.
const myList = new Proxy(List.of(1, 2, 3), historyHandler);

console.log('myList', myList.toJS());
// -> myList [ 1, 2, 3 ]
myList.push(4);
console.log('push(4)', myList.toJS());
// -> push(4) [ 1, 2, 3, 4 ]
myList.delete(0);
console.log('delete(0)', myList.toJS());
// -> delete(0) [ 2, 3, 4 ]
myList.undo();
console.log('undo()', myList.toJS());
// -> undo() [ 1, 2, 3, 4 ]
myList.undo();
console.log('undo()', myList.toJS());
// -> undo() [ 1, 2, 3 ]
```

There's a lot going on here, so let's unpack it. We'll start with the end result—an Immutable.js list augmented with history tracking capabilities:

```
const myList = new Proxy(List.of(1, 2, 3), historyHandler);

console.log('myList', myList.toJS());
// -> myList [ 1, 2, 3 ]
myList.push(4);
console.log('push(4)', myList.toJS());
// -> push(4) [ 1, 2, 3, 4 ]
myList.delete(0);
console.log('delete(0)', myList.toJS());
// -> delete(0) [ 2, 3, 4 ]
myList.undo();
console.log('undo()', myList.toJS());
// -> undo() [ 1, 2, 3, 4 ]
myList.undo();
console.log('undo()', myList.toJS());
// -> undo() [ 1, 2, 3 ]
```

The `Proxy` class—introduced to JavaScript in ES2015—is used as a mechanism to intercept anything that's called on the list that it wraps. We're mainly interested in the persistent change methods and the `undo()` method. As you can see, calling the `undo()` method on the list removes the most recent state of the collection. Here, we're making three changes, so calling `undo()` three times puts the list back in its original state.

To store the state of each collection after it has been changed, we're using `WeakMap`. The collection itself is the key, while the value is a stack of collections. Every time the collection changes, a new version of the collection is added to this stack. We also have a list of methods—these are the persistent change methods about which we care most. If it isn't in this list, then we don't care about it:

```
const persistentChanges = [
  'set',
  'delete',
  'deleteAll',
  'clear',
  'update',
  'merge',
  ...
];

const mutations = new WeakMap();
```

Then we have the proxy handler itself. It only defines a `get()` method. The idea is that it intercepts any method calls to the collection that you're wrapping. Then, you can decide what to do. You can either do nothing and simply forward the call to the collection, or you can forward the call to the collection and store the resulting new collection in its mutation stack.

The first step is getting the stack, which involves creating one if it doesn't exist:

```
if (!mutations.has(target)) {
  mutations.set(
    target,
    Stack().unshift(target)
  );
}

const stack = mutations.get(target);
```

Now that we have the mutation stack for the given collection, we're ready to figure out what to do with the requested key. We'll check if the caller wants a persistent change method: `persistentChanges.includes(key)`. If this is the case, then you can return a function that will push the result of the change (a new collection) onto the mutation stack:

```
return (...args) => {
  const result = stack.first()[key](...args);

  mutations.set(
    target,
    stack.unshift(result)
  );

  return result;
};
```

You call the method in question from the first instance of this collection in the mutation stack. The result then goes into the stack; so, the next time that you call a persistent change method, it'll be from this new collection.

If the caller is looking for the `undo()` method, we provide the following implementation from the proxy:

```
return () =>
  mutations.set(
    target,
    stack.count() > 1 ? stack.shift() : stack
  );
```

This pops the latest version off the mutation stack. For any other method that you try to call on this collection—anything that isn't a persistent change method or the `undo()` method—you just need to forward the call to the first collection in the mutation stack, since it is the latest version of the collection:

```
return stack.first()[key];
```

Is this a perfect solution or the only way to go in implementing history with immutable collections? It sure isn't, but it does what we need it to for now. In the future, you might decide only to keep so many versions of the collections to avoid memory leaks.

Summary

In this chapter, you learned about persistent change methods of Immutable.js collections. Each of these methods returns a new instance of the collection, but it retains any parts of the data that didn't actually change for efficiency purposes.

The types of persistent change methods include insertion, updates, removal, and emptying of entire collections. You saw how these methods can be chained together to handle more than one action at a time. Lastly, we took an in-depth look at managing the change history of collections and how immutability can contribute to the solution.

In the next chapter, we'll look at filtering collections.

Filtering Collections and Finding Items

4

Filtering collections is the most common operation performed with Immutable.js collections. Filters get us the parts of the collection that matter: the data that's relevant for the task at hand. There are only a handful of collection methods that are relevant to filtering collections and finding specific values, each of which can be used in many ways to get us the data that we need. In this chapter, you'll learn about the following:

- The basics of filtering Immutable.js collections
- Filtering maps based on their keys
- Finding specific collection values
- How deep equality in Immutable.js works
- Performing partial matches when searching
- Changing the search direction

Filtering using simple comparisons

Many of the filtering operations that you want to perform are simple ones. These include simple equality checks, greater than checks, and less than checks. Each of these comparisons is executed in a callback function that's passed to the `filter()` method.

Strict equality

Strict equality is used when you're looking for a value in a collection, and you have something with which you can compare it. For example, you could define a `filter` function that uses strict equality to look for values that equal 1 or 2, as follows:

```
const filter = i => i === 1 || i === 2;
```

You can then pass this function to the `filter()` method of a list:

```
const myList = List.of(1, 2, 3);
const myFilteredList = myList.filter(filter);

console.log('myList', myList.toJS());
// -> myList [ 1, 2, 3 ]
console.log('myFilteredList', myFilteredList.toJS());
// -> myFilteredList [ 1, 2 ]
```

You can use the same function to filter maps, as shown here:

```
const myMap = Map.of(
  'one', 1,
  'two', 2,
  'three', 3
);
const myFilteredMap = myMap.filter(filter);

console.log('myMap', myMap.toJS());
// -> myMap { one: 1, two: 2, three: 3 }
console.log('myFilteredMap', myFilteredMap.toJS());
// -> myFilteredMap { one: 1, two: 2 }
```

Note how the result of filtering a map is another map. This is difficult to do with plain JavaScript objects, even with the help of a library. With Immutable.js, you'll always get a map as the result.

Greater than and less than

Another type of simple comparison that you might want to perform when filtering collections is greater than or less than. Once again, this is done in the callback function that's passed to the `filter()` method:

```
const myList = List.of(1, 2, 3);
const myMap = Map.of(
  'one', 1,
  'two', 2,
  'three', 3
);
const myFilteredList = myList.filter(i => i < 3);
const myFilteredMap = myMap.filter(i => i > 1);

console.log('myList', myList.toJS());
// -> myList [ 1, 2, 3 ]
console.log('myFilteredList', myFilteredList.toJS());
// -> myFilteredList [ 1, 2 ]
console.log('myMap', myMap.toJS());
// -> myMap { one: 1, two: 2, three: 3 }
console.log('myFilteredMap', myFilteredMap.toJS());
// -> myFilteredMap { two: 2, three: 3 }
```

You can filter either list values or map values using greater than or less than operators. But what if you wanted to filter your collection to be within a range of values? You can construct a callback function, that makes sure that a given value is within a specified range, as follows:

```
const rangeFilter = (min, max) => v => v > min && v < max;
const myFilteredByRange = myList.filter(rangeFilter(1, 3));

console.log('myFilteredByRange', myFilteredByRange.toJS());
// -> myFilteredByRange [ 2 ]
```

The `rangeFilter()` function that we've implemented returns a new callback function that can be passed to the `filter()` method. You can give it a `min` and `max` value, which is then used to compare against each collection value—only values that fall between these two values are returned.

Filtering by negation

Sometimes, you only know the collection values that you don't want. Instead of building negation into your callback functions, you can use the `filterNot()` method, as follows:

```
const myMap = Map.of(
  'one', 1,
  'two', 2,
  'three', 3
);

const myFilter = i => i % 2;
const myOddsMap = myMap.filter(myFilter);
const myEvensMap = myMap.filterNot(myFilter);

console.log('myMap', myMap.toJS());
// -> myMap { one: 1, two: 2, three: 3 }
console.log('myOddsMap', myOddsMap.toJS());
// -> myOddsMap { one: 1, three: 3 }
console.log('myEvensMap', myEvensMap.toJS());
// -> myEvensMap { two: 2 }
```

What's nice about having two inverted filter functions such as `filter()` and `filterNot()` is that you can create a generic filter function, as we have done here with `myFilter()`. You can then toggle between values that you want and items that you don't want.

Filtering maps by keys

When filtering maps, it's helpful to be able to filter by keys. With lists, you're less likely to filter values by their indexes. Keys, on the other hand, usually have meaning within the context of your application.

Filtering string keys

Having maps with simple strings as keys is common. You can use them in your `filter()` callback functions because keys are passed as the second argument:

```
const myMap = Map.of(
  'one', 1,
  'two', 2,
  'three', 3
);
const myFilteredMap = myMap.filter(
```

```
  (v, k) => k.includes('o')
);

console.log('myMap', myMap.toJS());
// -> myMap { one: 1, two: 2, three: 3 }
console.log('myFilteredMap', myFilteredMap.toJS());
// -> myFilteredMap { one: 1, two: 2 }
```

As you can see, `myFilteredMap` only includes values whose keys include the letter o.

Filtering fancy keys

Unlike plain JavaScript objects, Immutable.js maps can use anything as a key. A common use of this capability is to associate data with a map that you don't necessarily want to add to the map as a value. You can then filter the map based on the maps used as keys:

```
const myFancyMap = Map.of(
  Map.of('name', 'one'), 1,
  Map.of('name', 'two'), 2,
  Map.of('name', 'three'), 3
);
const myFilteredMap = myFancyMap.filter(
  (v, k) => k.get('name').startsWith('t')
);

console.log('myFancyMap', myFancyMap.toJS());
// -> myFancyMap
// -> { 'Map { "name": "one" }': 1,
// ->   'Map { "name": "two" }': 2,
// ->   'Map { "name": "three" }': 3 }
console.log('myFilteredMap', myFilteredMap.toJS());
// -> myFilteredMap
// -> { 'Map { "name": "two" }': 2,
// ->   'Map { "name": "three" }': 3 }
```

There's really no limit to what you can filter with maps that have complex keys, such as other maps. In the preceding example, we got the numbers associated with keys that have a `name` property beginning with the letter t.

Finding collection values

Filtering collections is a good idea when you're not exactly sure what you'll find. At other times, you know that there's exactly one collection value needed. The problem with filtering is that the entire collection is searched no matter what. When you try to find a single item, the search ends with the first match.

Value existence checks

There are different types of existence checks that you can perform, depending on the type of collection. If it's a list, it's an indexed collection, which means that you can check for the existence of a specific index. If it's a map, it's a keyed collection, which means that you can check for the existence of a specific key. You can also check for the existence of a value in either collection type.

Let's create a list and check for some indexes, as follows:

```
const myList = List.of(1, 2, 3);
const myListHas2 = myList.has(2);
const myListHas3 = myList.has(3);

console.log('myListHas2', myListHas2);
// -> myListHas2 true
console.log('myListHas3', myListHas3);
// -> myListHas3 false
```

The myList collection has the index 2, but it doesn't have the index 3. Let's try the same thing with map keys now:

```
const myMap = Map.of(
  'one', 1,
  'two', 2,
  'three', 3
);
const myMapHasThree = myMap.has('three');
const myMapHasFour = myMap.has('four');

console.log('myMapHasThree', myMapHasThree);
// -> myMapHasThree true
console.log('myMapHasFour', myMapHasFour);
// -> myMapHasFour false
```

The `myMap` collection has the key `three`, but it doesn't have the key `four`. The `has()` method works the same way with lists and maps. You can check for the existence of values in collections using the `includes()` method. Here's what this looks like with lists:

```
const myListIncludes3 = myList.includes(3);
const myListIncludes4 = myList.includes(4);

console.log('myListIncludes3', myListIncludes3);
// -> myListIncludes3 true
console.log('myListIncludes4', myListIncludes4);
// -> myListIncludes4 false
```

Here, it returns `true` for the value 3 because it exists in the collection. It returns `false` for the value 4 because it isn't in the collection. Here's the same method used with maps:

```
const myMapIncludes3 = myMap.includes(3);
const myMapIncludes4 = myMap.includes(4);

console.log('myMapIncludes3', myMapIncludes3);
// -> myMapIncludes3 true
console.log('myMapIncludes4', myMapIncludes4);
// -> myMapIncludes4 false
```

Getting values using find()

The `find()` method lets you to search for a specific value in a collection. It works a lot like the `filter()` method, with two important differences:

- It doesn't return a new collection with the filtered results; it returns the value of what it finds
- It stops searching for values as soon as a match is found

The `find()` method takes the same callback function as the `filter()` method. You can find list values as follows:

```
const myList = List.of(1, 2, 3);
const myFoundListItem = myList.find(v => v === 3);
const myNotFoundListItem = myList.find(v => v === 4);

console.log('myFoundListItem', myFoundListItem);
// -> myFoundListItem 3
console.log('myNotFoundListItem', myNotFoundListItem);
// -> myNotFoundListItem undefined
```

You can also find map values:

```
const myMap = Map.of(
  'one', 1,
  'two', 2,
  'three', 3
);
const myFoundMapItem = myMap.find(v => v === 3);
const myNotFoundMapItem = myMap.find(v => v === 4);

console.log('myFoundMapItem', myFoundMapItem);
// -> myFoundMapItem 3
console.log('myNotFoundMapItem', myNotFoundMapItem);
// -> myNotFoundMapItem undefined
```

When no values are found by `find()`, the `undefined` value is returned. You can change this behavior by passing a third argument: `find(() => {}, null, 'myDefaultValue')`. The second parameter is the context for the predicate function, which can be ignored by passing `null`.

Filtering using deep equality

String equality works well when you need to compare two object references or two primitive values. But what about the cases where you want to compare something complex, such as two maps? Strict equality doesn't work here because they're two distinct references, even though their keys and values are the same. Immutable.js provides tools for performing deep collection comparisons.

Using the is() function and the equals() method

Immutable.js exports an `is()` function, which is used to compare two values. It can compare primitive JavaScript types using the same semantics as `Object.is()`, and it can do deep comparisons between two Immutable.js collections. When you pass two collections to `is()`, it will actually call the `equals()` method of the first collection. This means that you can be more direct if you know that you're comparing two collection types by calling `equals()`. If you don't know what you're comparing, `is()` is the better choice.

Let's start by comparing some lists:

```
const myList = List.of(1, 2);
console.log('myList', myList.toJS());
// -> myList [ 1, 2 ]
console.log('is([1, 2])', is(myList, List.of(1, 2)));
// -> is([1, 2]) true
console.log('equals([1, 2])', myList.equals(List.of(1, 2)));
// -> equals([1, 2]) true
console.log('is([1, 1])', is(myList, List.of(1, 1)));
// -> is([1, 1]) false
console.log('equals([1, 1])', myList.equals(List.of(1, 1)));
// -> equals([1, 1]) false
console.log('is([2, 1])', is(myList, List.of(2, 1)));
// -> is([2, 1]) false
console.log('equals([2, 1])', myList.equals(List.of(2, 1)));
// -> equals([2, 1]) false
```

Here, we're performing three comparisons; each are done using both `is()` and `equals()` so that you can see that there's no difference between them. When the list values are the same, you get a match. When the values are the same but the orders don't match, `is()` and `equals()` return `false`. A *list* is an ordered collection, and ordering is considered part of the equality. Deep equality checking with maps works the same way as it does with lists:

```
const myMap = Map.of('one', 1);
console.log('myMap', myMap.toJS());
// -> myMap { one: 1 }
console.log('is({ one: 1 })', is(myMap, Map.of('one', 1)));
// -> is({ one: 1 }) true
console.log('equals({ one: 1 })', myMap.equals(Map.of('one', 1)));
// -> equals({ one: 1 }) true
console.log('is({ two: 1 })', is(myMap, Map.of('two', 1)));
// -> is({ two: 1 }) false
console.log('equals({ two: 1 })', myMap.equals(Map.of('two', 1)));
// -> equals({ two: 1 }) false
console.log('is({ one: 2 })', is(myMap, Map.of('one', 2)));
// -> is({ one: 2 }) false
console.log('equals({ one: 1 })', myMap.equals(Map.of('one', 2)));
// -> equals({ one: 1 }) false
```

 The `equals()` method (called by `is()`) will recursively compare collections for equality. If you have a map with another map as a value, the collection you're comparing would need this same map property with the same values in order to be considered equal.

Searching lists of maps

Now that you know Immutable.js is capable of performing the heavy lifting involved with deep equality checking, let's see how it applies to searching collections. With some methods, you can simply pass the collection for which you want to search. This collection is then compared against every value in the other collection. Here's how this works with the `includes()` method:

```
const myList = List.of(
  Map.of('one', 1),
  Map.of('two', 2),
  Map.of('three', 3)
);
const includesOne = myList.includes(Map.of('one', 1));

console.log('includesOne', includesOne);
// -> includesOne true
```

The `includes()` method uses the `is()` function for comparisons. Since you're passing in a collection, you're ultimately calling the `equals()` method on every value in the collection until one of them returns `true`. What if you want to perform this type of deep equality check with the `filter()` function? You can't simply pass it a collection—it expects a predicate function. No problem—just do the following:

```
const is = a => b => a.equals(b);
```

With this handy little utility, you can compose predicate functions that do deep comparison of everything in the collection with whatever you pass to `is()`:

```
const myFilteredList = myList.filterNot(is(Map.of('one', 1)));

console.log('myFilteredList', myFilteredList.toJS());
// -> myFilteredList [ { two: 2 }, { three: 3 } ]
```

Remember, your version of `is()` returns a function to be used as a predicate with `filter()` or any other collection method that takes a predicate argument.

Partial matches

You won't always want to perform exact matches. Sometimes, you're looking for only one or two property values to match instead of every property value. For instance, a map might have two of the key-value pairs that you're looking for. But if this map has any other properties in which you're not interested, or that you don't know about, you can't match against it.

The shape of maps

A map has a particular **shape** if it has the key-value pairs that make up the shape. A person shape, for example, could be gender and age keys with specific values. If a map has these, it doesn't matter what other key-value pairs it has because you're not using them. With Immutable.js, performing partial matches to find values that fit a particular shape is commonplace. How do you perform deep equality checks only for specific key-value pairs? Let's find out.

Subsets and supersets

In the context of filtering collections, the map that acts as the shape that you're seeking is a potential **subset** of any value within the search space. If it's a subset, you know that the value fits the shape. Let's implement a function that will compose a predicate to check if one map is a subset of another map:

```
const mapIncludes = subset => superset =>
  subset
    .entrySeq()
    .map(List)
    .isSubset(
      superset
        .entrySeq()
        .map(List)
    );
```

The `subset` argument represents the shape that you're seeking. The `superset` argument represents the value in the collection that you're comparing against. We're converting both maps to lists of key-value pairs, then calling the `isSubset()` method to perform the actual comparison. Let's see `mapIncludes()` in action:

```
const myList = List.of(
  Map.of('one', 1, 'two', 2, 'three', 3),
  Map.of('one', 1, 'two', 2, 'four', 4),
  Map.of('one', 1, 'three', 3, 'four', 4)
);

// We can pass simple maps to compare, without the need
// to write a bunch of comparison logic.
const filteredOneTwo = myList.filter(
  mapIncludes(Map.of('one', 1, 'two', 2))
);
const filteredFourFive = myList.filter(
  mapIncludes(Map.of('four', 4, 'five', 5))
);

console.log('myList', myList.toJS());
// -> myList
// -> [ { one: 1, two: 2, three: 3 },
// ->   { one: 1, two: 2, four: 4 },
// ->   { one: 1, three: 3, four: 4 } ]
console.log('filteredOneTwo', filteredOneTwo.toJS());
// -> filteredOneTwo
// -> [ { one: 1, two: 2, three: 3 },
// ->   { one: 1, two: 2, four: 4 } ]
console.log('filteredFourFive', filteredFourFive.toJS());
// -> filteredFourFive []
```

Searching for maps that have the `one` and `two` key-value pairs produces results. The `three` and `four` key-value pairs are ignored. The second `filter()` call doesn't produce any results because the `five` key-value pair isn't included in any of the `myList` values.

Changing the search direction

By default, searching Immutable.js collections moves from left to right. This might not always be the best choice, so you have to think about changing the direction of your searches. There are a couple of ways to do this.

Searching sorted collections

The main reason that you would want to change the search direction is if the collection in question is sorted. For example, you want to find the oldest person in a list, or you want to filter the five oldest people in your list by some other criteria. It doesn't make sense to start at the beginning of the list if it's sorted in ascending order. You could reverse the list and then filter, but reversing a collection isn't free in terms of performance.

Using findLast() and reduceRight()

If there's a specific value you're looking for, starting from the end of the list and moving toward the beginning of it, you can use the `findLast()` method, as follows:

```
const myList = List.of('apples', 'bananas', 'cherries', 'chocolate');
const predicate = s => s.startsWith('ch');
const myFoundItem = myList.findLast(predicate);

console.log('myList', myList.toJS());
// -> myList [ 'apples', 'bananas', 'cherries', 'chocolate' ]
console.log('myFoundItem', myFoundItem);
// -> myFoundItem chocolate
```

As it turns out, the `predicate()` function finds a value at the very end of this list. Since you're starting at the end and moving left, no other values are checked. Let's use `predicate()` to perform a filter from the right:

```
const myFilteredList = myList.reduceRight(
  (result, v) => predicate(v) ?
    result.unshift(v) : result,
  List()
);

console.log('myFilteredList', myFilteredList.toJS());
// -> myFilteredList [ 'cherries', 'chocolate' ]
```

There's no `filterRight()` method in Immutable.js collections, so you have to create your own using `reduceRight()`. This method iterates over the collection from right to left like you want; you just have to call `predicate()` manually for each value and build the resulting list. Notice that we're using `unshift()` so that the order in the results is preserved.

Summary

In this chapter, we looked at filtering collections in Immutable.js. There are a number of ways to filter collections, including simple value comparisons and comparing the keys of maps. The `filter()` method is fundamental, and it's up to you to provide it with the appropriate predicate function.

We looked at finding values, which is similar to filtering except that it stops iterating over the collection once a match is found. You then learned about deep collection equality in Immutable.js. This is a common task when building applications, including the ability to perform partial deep equality checks. We also addressed the concept of searching in the opposite direction.

In the next chapter, we'll look at sequences and side-effects.

5
Sequences and Side-Effects

To make use of Immutable.js collections, you need to make use of sequences and side-effects. A **sequence** is a number of operations that apply to a collection to transform it. A **side-effect** is what we do with the result of a sequence to interact with the outside world. The reason that we structure our Immutable.js code like this is because it's efficient and readable. In this chapter, we will learn about the following:

- How Immutable.js can efficiently process large collections using lazy evaluation
- Creating sequences and studying how to iterate over them
- How lazy filtering works
- Limiting the data that's actually processed and used

Why lazy evaluation?

In Immutable.js, we use sequences to chain together transformation method calls. Using sequences this way, we're doing something called **lazy evaluation**; that is, we only process data from collections that actually need to be processed. Without lazy evaluation, we would have to process entire collections or come up with some other means to avoid processing work.

Large collections are expensive

A **large collection** is a collection that contains enough values that the cost of processing it becomes a cause for concern. Depending on the application—where it runs, who uses it, and how the collections are processed—a large collection could be anywhere from 500 to 10,000+ values.

Generally speaking, performing any kind of operation on a large collection only once isn't a big deal. The problem with this premise is that rarely do applications process collections only once. Often, the same collection is processed several times within the same function.

With Immutable.js collections, the cost of processing large collections is especially important because, since these collections are immutable, you're constantly creating and processing them.

Avoiding unnecessary work

The goal of using lazy evaluation is to avoid unnecessary work. When you're dealing with large collections, there are a lot of values that you don't need. Think about a user interface that displays a list. The source of the list is a collection of values. Since you're only displaying a small portion of this list in the UI, it doesn't make sense to process the whole thing.

Lazy evaluation avoids processing the entire collection by only processing one value at a time and on demand. The idea is that a side-effect is responsible for rendering this list in the UI. The side-effect knows that there is a need to display only 20 items in this list. As this side-effect iterates over a sequence of transformations, it asks the collection for a new value. Instead of iterating over 100,000 values, we'll never iterate over more than 20 values.

Chained operations are easy to understand

When you chain data transformation operations together, it's easy to examine the code and get a sense of what the end result will look like. With Immutable.js sequences, we get to keep this easy-to-maintain code structure, while sequences handle the underlying lazy evaluation. You don't have to think about passing individual collection values from one operation to the next—this all happens seamlessly.

Sequence creation and iteration

There are two ways to create sequences: you can directly create sequence instances, passing them collection data, or you can transform existing collections, such as lists and maps, into sequences.

Basic sequence creation

You can create new sequences by passing the `Seq()` constructor JavaScript arrays or objects, as follows:

```
import { Seq } from 'immutable';

const myIndexedSeq = Seq([1, 2, 3]);
const myKeyedSeq = Seq({ one: 1, two: 2, three: 3 });

console.log('myIndexedSeq', myIndexedSeq.toJS());
// -> myIndexedSeq [ 1, 2, 3 ]
console.log('myKeyedSeq', myKeyedSeq.toJS());
// -> myKeyedSeq { one: 1, two: 2, three: 3 }
```

There are actually two types of sequence collections: `Seq.Indexed` and `Seq.Keyed`. The `Seq()` constructor, which is really just a function due to the absence of the `new` keyword, will return the correct type of collection depending on what's passed to it.

 Generally speaking, you don't have to worry about the distinction between indexed and keyed sequence types. The best way to think about sequences is that `Seq.Indexed` is like a lazy `List` sequence type while `Seq.Keyed` is like a lazy `Map` sequence type.

Creating sequences directly like this isn't common, because they don't have the persistent change methods of other collections such as lists or maps. Sequences are for transforming data for immediate use, not mutating data for later use.

Collections to sequences

The common approach to sequence creation is to convert an existing collection into a sequence using the `toSeq()` method. Just like the `Seq()` constructor, `toSeq()` knows what type of sequence to create based on the type of collection that's being converted.

Another benefit of using `toSeq()` is that it fits nicely into the chained method call approach of Immutable.js: convert the collection to a sequence and then start calling transformation methods.

Lists to sequences

We can convert lists to sequences using `toSeq()`, as shown here:

```
const myList = List.of(1, 2, 3);
const myIndexedSeq = myList.toSeq();

console.log('myIndexedSeq', myIndexedSeq.toJS());
// -> myIndexedSeq [ 1, 2, 3 ]
```

Maps to sequences

We can convert maps to sequences using `toSeq()`:

```
const myMap = Map.of(
  'one', 1,
  'two', 2,
  'three', 3
);
const myKeyedSeq = myMap.toSeq();

console.log('myKeyedSeq', myKeyedSeq.toJS());
// -> myKeyedSeq { one: 1, two: 2, three: 3 }
```

 These examples aim to illustrate that sequences are simply a representation of the original collection. It's not often that you'll store sequences in constants like this. In fact, there are several places in this book where we store constants unnecessarily. This is done simply as an effort to make the code more teachable.

Iterating with for...of loops

Immutable.js collections follow the JavaScript **iterable protocol**. Any object that follows it can be used in a `for...of` loop. This includes sequences, as shown here:

```
const myList = List.of(1, 2, 3);
const myMap = Map.of(
  'one', 1,
  'two', 2,
  'three', 3
);

for (let item of myList.toSeq()) {
  console.log('myList', item);
```

```
  // -> myList 1
  // -> myList 2
  // -> myList 3
}

for (let item of myMap.toSeq()) {
  console.log('myMap', item);
  // -> myMap [ 'one', 1 ]
  // -> myMap [ 'two', 2 ]
  // -> myMap [ 'three', 3 ]
}
```

Here, we're converting `myList` and `myMap` into their respective sequence types using `toSeq()`. Then, we're iterating over each value inside of a `for...of` loop. This is a side-effect: we're iterating over a sequence in order to communicate with the outside world using `console.log()`. Technically, we didn't actually have to use `toSeq()` here. The iterable behavior would have worked just fine with lists or maps.

Iterating with forEach()

As an alternative to `for...of` loops, the `forEach()` method can be used by sequences to execute side-effects, as follows:

```
const myList = List.of(1, 2, 3);
const myMap = Map.of(
  'one', 1,
  'two', 2,
  'three', 3
);

myList
  .toSeq()
  .forEach(item => console.log('myList', item));
  // -> myList 1
  // -> myList 2
  // -> myList 3

myMap
  .toSeq()
  .forEach(item => console.log('myMap', item));
  // -> myMap 1
  // -> myMap 2
  // -> myMap 3
```

Using this approach, we end up with the same result as using `for...of` loops to execute our side-effects. The `toSeq()` call isn't necessary in order to use `forEach()`; however, the advantage that it has over `for...of` loops is that it's a chainable method that can be attached to your sequence transformations. This means fewer constants without sacrificing code readability.

Lazy filtering

We've seen multiple ways to build sequences so far—now let's introduce a real need for them. When you filter sequences, each value from the collection is passed through the predicate function and into the side-effect, one at a time.

Basic lazy filtering

To help illustrate the concept of lazy filtering, let's implement a basic predicate function with some extra logging:

```
const predicate = (item) => {
  console.log('filtering', item);
  return item % 2;
};
```

This logging will make it easy for us to see when the actual filtering of a value happens relative to when the value is used in the side-effect. Let's try this on an indexed sequence:

```
const myList = List.of(1, 2, 3, 4, 5, 6);
myList
  .toSeq()
  .filter(predicate)
  .forEach(item => console.log('myList', item));
// -> filtering 1
// -> myList 1
// -> filtering 2
// -> filtering 3
// -> myList 3
// -> filtering 4
// -> filtering 5
// -> myList 5
// -> filtering 6
```

If you pay close attention to the output, you can see that the ordering of the logs reflects the lazy nature of sequences. The filtering logs are interwoven with the logs produced from the side-effect. You would never log from a predicate like this in practice—we're only doing it here to show the ordering of sequence operations. Let's try the same sequence approach with a keyed sequence:

```
myMap
    .toSeq()
    .filter(predicate)
    .forEach(item => console.log('myMap', item));
    // -> filtering 1
    // -> myMap 1
    // -> filtering 2
    // -> filtering 3
    // -> myMap 3
    // -> filtering 4
    // -> filtering 5
    // -> myMap 5
    // -> filtering 6
```

You get the same result as before with indexed sequences—lazily evaluated filter predicates. As the `forEach()` method iterates over the sequence, it asks for the result from the next method in the chain. The `filter()` method then iterates over the sequence until a match is found, pauses, and waits for the next iteration from `forEach()`.

Eager evaluation is the opposite of lazy evaluation. To see eager evaluation in action, comment out the call to `toSeq()` in the preceding examples, and pay attention to the output. All of the filtering logs will come before logs from the side-effect because they're evaluated eagerly.

Multiple filter levels

Let's see how lazy evaluation works with more than one sequence operation. To do so, let's first implement a function to compose filter predicates, as follows:

```
const equals = first => (second) => {
    console.log(`${first} === ${second}`);
    return first === second;
};
```

Now we have an easy way to build a simple predicate that logs what we're comparing and then returns the result of the actual comparison. Let's put `equals()` to use by chaining together several filters:

```
myList
  .toSeq()
  .filterNot(equals(1))
  .filterNot(equals(3))
  .filterNot(equals(5))
  .forEach(item => console.log('myList', item));
// -> 1 === 1
// -> 1 === 2
// -> 3 === 2
// -> 5 === 2
// -> myList 2
// -> 1 === 3
// -> 3 === 3
// -> 1 === 4
// -> 3 === 4
// -> 5 === 4
// -> myList 4
// -> 1 === 5
// -> 3 === 5
// -> 5 === 5
// -> 1 === 6
// -> 3 === 6
// -> 5 === 6
// -> myList 6
```

There are three calls to `filterNot()` chained together here. Remember that `filterNot()` is just like `filter()`, except that it negates the result. The end result is that we don't want any values that equal 1, 3, or 5.

Let's look at the output. You can see that the pattern on the left-hand side of the `===` operator repeats in the order of the values that we've passed to `filterNot(equals())`. The first call to `filterNot()` defers to the second call and so on. The consequence of lazy evaluation done this way is that `filterNot()` is never applied to an entire collection at once, and we don't need to allocate new collections as values flow through the sequence operations.

The cherry on top of all of this is that you can break your predicate logic down into concise reusable units. The example we've just walked through illustrates this point. Instead of having one predicate function handle every filter case, you can keep your predicates focused on just one thing and chain them together with no significant performance penalty.

Limiting results and reducing work

You've seen how to chain sequence operations together. By doing this, you can pass one value at a time to your chain and into your side-effect. This lets you write legible code that doesn't create intermediary collections between operations. However, you can still run into performance problems with large collections because you'll still have to iterate over every value.

Using take() to limit results

Use the `take()` method to tell sequences that you only want a specific number of results. For example, if a page in your application wants to display 20 values, you could add `take(20)` to your sequence chain. Where should you add this call? The order of where `take()` is placed in the chain of method calls can have dramatic effects on the result.

Let's start by creating an infinite sequence, as shown in the following code block:

```
import { Range } from 'immutable';

const myRange = Range();
```

Here, `Range` is a special type of sequence that's handy for creating large sequences of numbers. Now let's create a predicate function to include only odd numbers:

```
const predicate = i => i % 2;
```

Let's see what happens when we place `take` before `filter`:

```
myRange
  .take(5)
  .filter(predicate)
  .forEach((item) => {
    console.log('myRange (take then filter)', item);
  });
// -> myRange (take then filter) 1
// -> myRange (take then filter) 3
```

This result is misleading—we wanted five values and only got two! This is because we took five items and then filtered them. What we really wanted was the first five values that passed through `filter()`. This just needs an order change:

```
myRange
  .filter(predicate)
  .take(5)
  .forEach((item) => {
    console.log('myRange (filter then take)', item);
  });
// -> myRange (filter then take) 1
// -> myRange (filter then take) 3
// -> myRange (filter then take) 5
// -> myRange (filter then take) 7
// -> myRange (filter then take) 9
```

By moving `take()` after `filter()` we get the result that we're after. Each `forEach()` iteration passes through the `take()` call to the `filter()` call. Once the limit is reached, we stop iterating.

This is how you perform lazy evaluation on large collections—you use sequences to avoid intermediate collections and any unnecessary work.

Using slice() to paginate

If you want to implement pagination, you can use the `slice()` method. This method works just like `take()`, except that it accepts an offset to start slicing values from a collection:

```
const predicate = i => i % 2 === 0;
const myRange = Range().filter(predicate);

const page1 = myRange.slice(0, 5);
const page2 = myRange.slice(5, 10);
const page3 = myRange.slice(10, 15);

page1.forEach(i => console.log('page1', i));
// -> page1 0
// -> page1 2
// -> page1 4
// -> page1 6
// -> page1 8

page2.forEach(i => console.log('page2', i));
// -> page2 10
// -> page2 12
```

```
// -> page2 14
// -> page2 16
// -> page2 18

page3.forEach(i => console.log('page3', i));
// -> page3 20
// -> page3 22
// -> page3 24
// -> page3 26
// -> page3 28
```

We've created three pages here: `page1`, `page2`, and `page3`. Since these are all sequences, the `slice()` method doesn't actually execute anything, including the `filter()` method that looks for even numbers. Once the `forEach()` side-effect is called on each of these pages, the `filter()` method is run for each item that `slice()` has requested.

Summary

In this chapter, we looked at sequences and lazy evaluation, as these concepts are central to Immutable.js. Lazy evaluation is especially important in scenarios where you have large collections, and having to process every value could result in performance issues.

Side-effects are how you initiate lazy evaluation of sequences. You can manually iterate over them, or you can use the `forEach()` method. Filtering sequences is also done lazily, even chaining together multiple filters. Since the lazy aspect of sequences is handled internally by Immutable.js, you can focus on readable method call chains.

Also, it's important for your side-effects to ask for a limited number of values from sequences, using `slice()` or `take()`, so that you can maximize the benefit of lazy evaluation.

In the next chapter, we'll look at sorting your collections.

6
Sorting Collections

Sorting collections is a common task in any application. With Immutable.js, sorting collections results in a new collection because nothing can change. Collections in Immutable.js provide us with a number of tools to handle sorting collections. In this chapter, we'll learn about the following:

- Basic sorting and reversing capabilities of collections
- Advanced sorting abilities with complex sort conditions
- The difference between ordered maps and sorting map values
- Maintaining the sort order of collections

Sorting and reversing

Just like the native JavaScript array, Immutable.js collections have a sort() method. Instead of sorting the values in place like an array, this results in a new collection.

The sort() method

Sorting lists is just like sorting native JavaScript arrays, except that you end up with a new list. The sort() method takes a **comparator** function, which is used to compare two collection values. If you don't provide this argument, the default comparator uses greater than and less than operators since this is the most common way to sort values:

```
const myList = List.of(2, 1, 4, 3);
const mySortedList = myList.sort();

console.log('myList', myList.toJS());
// -> myList [ 2, 1, 4, 3 ]
```

```
console.log('mySortedList', mySortedList.toJS());
// -> mySortedList [ 1, 2, 3, 4 ]
```

As you can see, the new list of numbers is created and it is sorted numerically.

 Sorting is one operation that can't be performed lazily, since you have to go through every item in the collection before you know what should be displayed first. Always sort collections before transforming them into sequences using `toSeq()`.

The reverse() method

Another method shared between native JavaScript arrays and Immutable.js lists is `reverse()`. It shares the same semantics as well: it reverses the current value order. This means that if you want the values sorted in reverse order, you have to sort them first:

```
const myList = List.of(2, 1, 4, 3);
const myReversedList = myList.reverse();

console.log('myList', myList.toJS());
// -> myList [ 2, 1, 4, 3 ]

console.log('myReversedList', myReversedList.toJS());
// -> myReversedList [ 3, 4, 1, 2 ]
```

This probably isn't what you're after. Since the list wasn't sorted before it was reversed, it doesn't end up in descending order. One answer is to call `sort()` and `reverse()`:

```
const mySortedReversedList = myList.sort().reverse();
console.log('mySortedReversedList', mySortedReversedList.toJS());
// -> mySortedReversedList [ 4, 3, 2, 1 ]
```

Another approach to sorting lists in descending order is to provide an iteratee argument to `sortBy()`:

```
const myBackwardSortedList = myList.sortBy(i => -i);
console.log('myBackwardSortedList', myBackwardSortedList.toJS());
// -> myBackwardSortedList [ 4, 3, 2, 1 ]
```

Since we know that our collection is filled with number values, we can use the `sortBy()` method to negate every value before it's sorted.

Sorting lists of maps

You've seen how to use the sortBy() method to negate a value so that you can sort in descending order. The sortBy() method is also useful when you need to sort by more complex data and sort criteria. Even the sortBy() method has its limitations with respect to sorting lists of maps; so, you have to think about alternative approaches here.

The sortBy() method

The sortBy() method uses the default greater than and less than comparator function—the same default used by sort(). The function that is passed to sortBy() is called an **iteratee**, which is a function that's used to produce values that are fed into the comparator function. This is useful when you want to use the default comparator—writing iteratees is easier than customizing comparator functions.

> If it turns out that you've written an iteratee function and you have a reusable comparator function, you can use both. The sortBy() method accepts a comparator as its second argument.

Let's start by writing a simple utility that helps us compose iteratee functions for maps:

```
const prop = p => map => map.get(p);
```

Here the prop() function takes a key and returns a function, which returns the value of the key for a given map. Now that we have a way to build an iteratee function, let's use it with sortBy():

```
const myList = List.of(
  Map.of('name', 'ccc', 'age', 23),
  Map.of('name', 'aaa', 'age', 23),
  Map.of('name', 'ddd', 'age', 19),
  Map.of('name', 'bbb', 'age', 19)
);
const byAge = myList
  .sortBy(prop('age'));

console.log('myList', myList.toJS());
// -> myList
// -> [ { name: 'ccc', age: 23 },
// ->   { name: 'aaa', age: 23 },
// ->   { name: 'ddd', age: 19 },
// ->   { name: 'bbb', age: 19 } ]
```

```
console.log('byAge', byAge.toJS());
// -> byAge
// -> [ { name: 'ddd', age: 19 },
// ->   { name: 'bbb', age: 19 },
// ->   { name: 'ccc', age: 23 },
// ->   { name: 'aaa', age: 23 } ]
```

The iteratee function that we created by calling prop('age') was passed to sortBy(). This returned the age value for every map in the list, and this is what was used by the comparator.

Sorting by multiple keys

What if you want to sort by both the age and name keys? For example, you want to sort by the age key first. However, there are several maps that have the same age value. This is where you want to compare the name keys. Using sortBy() for this is out of the question because you can't implement this using a single comparison. You have to implement your own comparator function, as follows:

```
const comp = (order, ...props) => (a, b) => {
  for (const p of props) {
    if (a.get(p) > b.get(p)) {
      return order * 1;
    }
    if (a.get(p) < b.get(p)) {
      return order * -1;
    }
  }
  return 0;
};
const asc = (...props) => comp(1, ...props);
const desc = (...props) => comp(-1, ...props);
```

The comp() function takes an order argument, either 1 for ascending or -1 for descending. It also accepts a number of map keys to compare. The order in which these keys are passed will determine the order in which they're used to sort the list. For example, the first key is used to sort everything, the second key is used as a tie-breaker for the first key, the third key is used as a tie-breaker for the second key, and so on.

The returned function is the new comparator that's used with `sort()`. The `order` argument inverts the number that's returned based on a greater than and less than comparison. Instead of having to remember to pass 1 or -1 to `comp()`, you have the `asc()` and `desc()` functions that do this:

```
const byAgeAndName = myList
  .sort(asc('age', 'name'));
const byAgeAndNameDesc = myList
  .sort(desc('age', 'name'));

console.log('byAgeAndName', byAgeAndName.toJS());
// -> byAgeAndName [ { name: 'ccc', age: 23 }
// ->               { name: 'aaa', age: 23 },
// ->               { name: 'ddd', age: 19 },
// ->               { name: 'bbb', age: 19 } ]

console.log('byAgeAndNameDesc', byAgeAndNameDesc.toJS());
// -> byAgeAndNameDesc [ { name: 'bbb', age: 19 },
// ->                   { name: 'ddd', age: 19 },
// ->                   { name: 'aaa', age: 23 },
// ->                   { name: 'ccc', age: 23 } ]
```

As you can see, the sort direction of both the `name` and `key` properties are reflected in the output, depending on whether the `asc()` or `desc()` function was used as the comparator.

Ordered maps

Maps don't preserve order the way that lists do. When you push a value to a list, the value will always be in the same position because lists are indexed. With maps, the order of a particular value doesn't matter because you can look it up by its key. When you're iterating over maps, ordering can become a problem though.

Order guarantees

The ordering of list values is guaranteed because lists are an indexed collection. Maps are a keyed collection, which means that the order in which key-value pairs are added isn't guaranteed to be preserved. For example, let's say that I call `myMap.set('one', 1).set('two', 2)`. If you were to iterate over this map, `one` would probably come before `two`. But this is misleading, because there are no ordering guarantees when it comes to iterating over maps. This could be a problem if your application expects iteration ordering to be consistent.

Insertion order is not sort order

The answer to the iteration order problem with maps is to use an **ordered map**. These maps preserve the order of values as they're inserted into the collection, just like lists. In fact, an ordered map behaves both like a keyed collection and an indexed collection. You can still find values using a key, and the iteration behavior works just like an indexed collection.

The name "ordered map" can be a little misleading. It implies that by adding a value, it's added in some kind of sort order. This isn't the case at all. There's nothing special about ordered maps other than that, internally, they maintain an index so that when you iterate over the map, strict ordering is defined.

Setting the order with set()

Let's look at what happens when you iterate over a map:

```
const myMap = Map()
  .set('one', 1)
  .set('two', 2)
  .set('three', 3);

myMap
  .forEach(i => console.log('myMap', i));
  // -> myMap 1
  // -> myMap 2
  // -> myMap 3
```

The iteration order is the same as the order in which you set the values. However, this iteration order isn't guaranteed. You could see a different order the next time you iterate over `myMap`. Let's try this with an ordered map now:

```
const myOrderedMap = OrderedMap()
  .set('three', 3)
  .set('two', 2)
  .set('one', 1);

myOrderedMap
  .forEach(i => console.log('myOrderedMap', i));
  // -> myOrderedMap 3
  // -> myOrderedMap 2
  // -> myOrderedMap 1
```

Our map, `myOrderedMap`, will always have the same iteration order. The order is defined as the order in which items are set. Since we're setting the value 3 first, it has an index of 0 (internally) and a key of `three`. If you were iterating over this map to render data in a user interface, consistent iteration order is important—the `OrderedMap` collections provide this guarantee.

Sorting maps

Just like lists, maps can be sorted too. To preserve the new order of the map once it's sorted, you have to convert it to an ordered map. You can also sort maps by their keys.

Creating ordered maps

Maps have a `sort()` method, just like lists. They even use the same default comparator function. To preserve the order of the map after `sort()` has been called, you can use `toOrderedMap()` to convert it, as follows:

```
const myMap = Map.of(
    'three', 3,
    'one', 1,
    'four', 4,
    'two', 2
);
const mySortedMap = myMap
    .toOrderedMap()
    .sort();

myMap.forEach(
    (v, k) => console.log('myMap', `${k} => ${v}`)
);
// -> myMap three => 3
// -> myMap one => 1
// -> myMap four => 4
// -&gt; myMap two => 2

mySortedMap.forEach(
    (v, k) => console.log('mySortedMap', `${k} => ${v}`)
);
// -> mySortedMap one => 1
// -> mySortedMap two => 2
// -> mySortedMap three => 3
// -> mySortedMap four => 4
```

The semantics of sort() are the same for lists and maps, as you can see by the sorted output. The iteration order of mySortedMap will always be the same, because it's an OrderedMap. When the sort happens, a new ordered map is created with the values in the expected order and an internal index to guarantee iteration order.

 If you're calling sort() on a Map, the toOrderedMap() call isn't needed because an OrderedMap instance is returned. On the other hand, there's no real downside to including the call, and it serves to communicate intent.

Sorting maps by key

Let's use the same approach—converting maps to ordered maps before sorting—to sort our maps by keys:

```
const mySortedByKeyMap = myMap
  .toOrderedMap()
  .sortBy((v, k) => k);

mySortedByKeyMap.forEach(
  (v, k) => console.log('mySortedByKeyMap', `${k} => ${v}`)
);
// -> mySortedByKeyMap four => 4
// -> mySortedByKeyMap one => 1
// -> mySortedByKeyMap three => 3
// -> mySortedByKeyMap two => 2
```

To sort maps by keys, you can use the sortBy() method to provide an iteratee function that returns the keys. This way, the keys are used by the comparator. The result, as you can see, is that the keys determine the sort order instead of the value.

Maintaining sort order

If your application has collections that are always sorted, then you need a way to maintain that sort order. This means that once you add or change values in a collection, you have to make sure that the collection is still in the order that you expected.

Finding the insertion index

Let's say that you want to add a value to a list that's already sorted. Using push() will insert the value at the end of the list, and this isn't what you want. The insert() method can put the value at a particular index—you just have to figure out which index to use to keep the list sorted:

```
const sortedInsert = (item, list) => {
  let low = 0;
  let high = list.count();

  while (low < high) {
    const mid = (low + high) >>> 1;
    if (item > list.get(mid)) {
      low = mid + 1;
    } else {
      high = mid;
    }
  }
  return list.insert(low, item);
};
```

The sortedIndex() function takes a value and a list into which to insert the value as arguments. It then does a simple binary search to find the correct index that will maintain the sort order of the collection. Let's see how this function works in practice:

```
const myList = List.of(1, 3, 5);
const withTwo = sortedInsert(2, myList);
const withFour = sortedInsert(4, withTwo);

console.log('myList', myList.toJS());
// -> myList [ 1, 3, 5 ]
console.log('withTwo', withTwo.toJS());
// -> withTwo [ 1, 2, 3, 5 ]
console.log('withFour', withFour.toJS());
// -> withFour [ 1, 2, 3, 4, 5 ]
```

The withTwo list has the value 2 inserted in the correct position, and withFour has 4 in the correct position. The main advantage of implementing this approach is that you can avoid having to re-sort the entire collection after pushing a new value. Finding the correct insertion index to maintain the sort order isn't without it's downsides, though.

Is this really necessary?

There are some questions that you should ask yourself before going down the insertion index path:

- Do I want to maintain my own insertion index functionality?
- What about the case where list values change?
- Is there anything actually wrong with sorting the collection after persistent changes?
- Do I just sort on the fly as part of the sequence and side-effect workflow?

Maintaining the sort order of collections by finding the insertion index for new or changed values is harder than sorting the collection. You can sort the collection every time you push new values or change existing values:

```
const usingSort = myList
  .push(2)
  .push(4)
  .sort();

console.log('usingSort', usingSort.toJS());
// -> usingSort [ 1, 2, 3, 4, 5 ]
```

The rule of thumb to follow here is just use sort() or sortBy(), unless there are compelling performance reasons that justify using the insertion index approach.

Summary

In this chapter, you learned about the basics of sorting collections in Immutable.js. The basic sort() and reverse() methods sort values using a default comparator function. You can supply your own comparator functions for more complex scenarios. There's also the sortBy() method that accepts an iteratee function, which is used to return values that are passed to the comparator.

We then addressed the issue of sorting maps. Because they're a keyed collection, they have no inherent mechanism to keep track of the order of values. Lists, on the other hand, have this value built into them. Ordered maps are used to preserve the ordering of maps. You can also sort maps by keys if you use sortBy() to return the key.

We looked at the problem of maintaining the sort order of collections. Having to sort collections every time they change can be inefficient. To address this, you can leverage the sort index approach. On the other hand, this can be difficult to maintain and `sort()` is good enough for most things.

In the next chapter, we'll look at mapping and reducing Immutable.js collections.

7
Mapping and Reducing

In this chapter, we'll look at mapping and reducing with Immutable.js collections. These are fundamental operations in any Immutable.js application. In particular, you'll learn how to do the following:

- Perform basic mapping operations to produce simple values
- Use complex mapping techniques that add new keys to maps and remove unwanted keys
- Reduce collections to simpler values when basic filtering isn't enough
- Lazily filter and map collections for the ultimate lazy pattern

Mapping lists of maps

Lists of maps are common in Immutable.js applications. Also common is the need to map these lists to lists of simple values. This means taking a simple value from the map, or using the map to compute a simple value.

Plucking values

Plucking a value from a map is another way of saying look up a value based on a key. It's common to say "pluck" when mapping a collection of maps to a particular key. Imagine plucking blades of grass from a lawn that fit a particular profile. Let's look at an example:

```
const myList = List.of(
  Map.of('first', 1, 'second', 2),
  Map.of('first', 3, 'second', 4),
  Map.of('first', 5, 'second', 6)
);
```

```
const myMappedList = myList
  .map(v => v.get('second'));

console.log('myList', myList.toJS());
// -> myList [ { first: 1, second: 2 },
// ->          { first: 3, second: 4 },
// ->          { first: 5, second: 6 } ]
console.log('myMappedList', myMappedList.toJS());
// -> myMappedList [ 2, 4, 6 ]
```

The `myMappedList` list now has the values of the `second` key. The iteratee (value mapper function) function used with `map()` returns the value by calling `get('second')`.

Computing new values

You can pass iteratee functions to `map()` that compute new values. Let's implement a function that capitalizes the string that's passed to it:

```
const capitalize = s =>
  `${s.charAt(0).toUpperCase()}${s.slice(1)}`;
```

This function will make the first character of any string uppercase. Let's use this as part of an iteratee function passed to `map()` to help generate a list of names:

```
const myList = List.of(
  Map.of('first', 'joe', 'last', 'brown', 'age', 45),
  Map.of('first', 'john', 'last', 'smith', 'age', 32),
  Map.of('first', 'mary', 'last', 'wise', 'age', 56)
);
const myMappedList = myList.map(
  v => [
    capitalize(v.get('first')),
    capitalize(v.get('last'))
  ].join(' ')
);

console.log('myList', myList.toJS());
// -> myList [ { first: 'joe', last: 'brown', age: 45 },
// ->          { first: 'john', last: 'smith', age: 32 },
// ->          { first: 'mary', last: 'wise', age: 56 } ]
console.log('myMappedList', myMappedList.toJS());
// -> myMappedList [ 'Joe Brown', 'John Smith', 'Mary Wise' ]
```

Our list is filled with maps that each have the `first` and `last` keys. We want to map each of these maps to a string consisting of the capitalized first and last names. The iteratee does this using the `capitalize()` function and putting the results into an array so that we can join them together. The result is a new list of name strings.

Mapping to new lists of maps

You don't always want to transform lists of maps into lists of simple values. Sometimes, you want to add new keys, remove existing keys, or both.

Creating new keys

Let's revisit the earlier example where we mapped a list of names. We'll do the same thing here, except that we'll add the resulting string to each map as a new key-value pair:

```
const capitalize = s =>
  `${s.charAt(0).toUpperCase()}${s.slice(1)}`;
const myList = List.of(
  Map.of('first', 'joe', 'last', 'brown', 'age', 45),
  Map.of('first', 'john', 'last', 'smith', 'age', 32),
  Map.of('first', 'mary', 'last', 'wise', 'age', 56)
);
const myMappedList = myList.map(
  v => v.set('name', [
    capitalize(v.get('first')),
    capitalize(v.get('last'))
  ].join(' '))
);

console.log('myList', myList.toJS());
// -> myList [ { first: 'joe', last: 'brown', age: 45 },
// ->          { first: 'john', last: 'smith', age: 32 },
// ->          { first: 'mary', last: 'wise', age: 56 } ]

console.log('myMappedList', myMappedList.toJS());
// -> myMappedList [ { first: 'joe', last: 'brown', age: 45, name: 'Joe
Brown' },
// ->               { first: 'john', last: 'smith', age: 32, name: 'John
Smith' },
// ->               { first: 'mary', last: 'wise', age: 56, name: 'Mary
Wise' } ]
```

Instead of returning the resulting string from our `map()` iteratee, we're returning a new map instance by calling `set()`. The new list of maps each have a `name` key now.

 This type of mapping is useful if you already have code that processes lists of maps and it expects a `name` key. You can easily add the key rather than change the list processing code.

Filtering keys

You can use `map()` to transform a list of maps into one that only has the keys that you need. To do this, you can implement a couple of utility functions that compose iteratees for you, as follows:

```
const pick = (...props) => map => map
  .filter((v, k) => props.includes(k));
const omit = (...props) => map => map
  .filterNot((v, k) => props.includes(k));
```

The `pick()` function returns an iteratee that will return a map that only includes the keys that are passed to `pick()`. The `omit()` function is the inverse of `pick()`—it will include everything except the keys passed to `omit()`. Let's see how they work here:

```
const myList = List.of(
  Map.of('first', 'joe', 'last', 'brown', 'age', 45),
  Map.of('first', 'john', 'last', 'smith', 'age', 32),
  Map.of('first', 'mary', 'last', 'wise', 'age', 56)
);
const myPickedList = myList.map(pick('first', 'last'));
const myOmittedList = myList.map(omit('first', 'last'));

console.log('myList', myList.toJS());
// -> myList [ { first: 'joe', last: 'brown', age: 45 },
// ->          { first: 'john', last: 'smith', age: 32 },
// ->          { first: 'mary', last: 'wise', age: 56 } ]

console.log('myPickedList', myPickedList.toJS());
// -> myPickedList [ { first: 'joe', last: 'brown' },
// ->                { first: 'john', last: 'smith' },
// ->                { first: 'mary', last: 'wise' } ]

console.log('myOmittedList', myOmittedList.toJS());
// -> myOmittedList [ { age: 45 },
// ->                 { age: 32 },
// ->                 { age: 56 } ]
```

You can see that `myPickedList` only includes the keys that were passed to `pick()` and `myOmittedList`. It doesn't include any keys that were passed to `omit()`.

Reducing collections

When you map collections, you always end up with the same type of collection with the same number of values. When you iterate over every value in the collection and produce something that's not a mapped collection, it's called a **reduction**. Filtering is a type of reduction, for example, but sometimes, you need to produce noncollection values from collections.

When filtering isn't enough

If you need to produce another collection, combining `filter()` and `map()` is usually the right answer. You can compose your `filter()` and `map()` calls using concise and easy to read iteratee functions. When you need to produce a simple value, the `reduce()` method is there for you.

 Manually reducing collections using `reduce()` requires more implementation effort than either `map()` and `filter()`, which is why you should avoid it where possible. Another reason to avoid it is that it can't be executed lazily in a sequence.

Producing minimums and maximums

An example of where mapping and filtering collections would be insufficient is finding minimum and maximum values. Let's implement some reducers to find these values in a collection:

```
const myList = List.of(
  Map.of('red', 3, 'black', 4),
  Map.of('red', 6, 'black', 8),
  Map.of('red', 9, 'black', 12)
);
const minRedReduce = myList.reduce(
  (result, v) => v.get('red') < result ?
    v.get('red') :
    result,
  myList.first().get('red')
);
```

```
const maxRedReduce = myList.reduce(
  (result, v) => v.get('red') > result ?
    v.get('red') :
    result,
  myList.first().get('red')
);

console.log('minRedReduce', minRedReduce);
// -> minRedReduce 3
console.log('maxRedReduce', maxRedReduce);
// -> maxRedReduce 9
```

The `result` argument that's passed to the iteratee is the reduction. The value returned by the iteratee is passed to the next iteratee as the `result` argument. The value that's returned is based on a simple comparison—do we have a new minimum or maximum? If so, return it. If not, return the current minimum or maximum.

Let's look at another approach to finding the minimum and maximum values from a collection:

```
const minRedMap = myList
  .map(v => v.get('red'))
  .min();
const maxRedMap = myList
  .map(v => v.get('red'))
  .max();

console.log('minRedMap', minRedMap);
// -> minRedMap 3
console.log('maxRedMap', maxRedMap);
// -> maxRedMap 9
```

Here, we're using two built-in reducer methods of Immutable.js—`min()` and `max()`. Before you can use them, however, you have to map your list of maps to a list of simple numerical values. There is one more approach to look at:

```
const minByRed = myList
  .minBy(v => v.get('red'))
  .get('red');
const maxByRed = myList
  .maxBy(v => v.get('red'))
  .get('red');

console.log('minByRed', minByRed);
// -> minByRed 3
console.log('maxByRed', maxByRed);
// -> maxByRed 9
```

The `minBy()` and `maxBy()` methods are also reducers. They each accept an iteratee function that determines the value to compare and reduce the minimum or maximum value. Another advantage to this approach is that you might not care what the actual minimum or maximum value is, only which map in your list is the minimum or maximum defined by some iteratee function that you provide.

Accumulating values

Basic arithmetic is another use of reducers. In the preceding section, we looked at minimums and maximums—the reduction is produced by performing comparisons. With accumulators, we're just changing the reduction based on simple addition and other operators. Let's take a look at some basic accumulators:

```
const myList = List.of(
  Map.of('red', 3, 'black', 4),
  Map.of('red', 6, 'black', 8),
  Map.of('red', 9, 'black', 12)
);
const redSum = myList.reduce(
  (result, v) => result + v.get('red'),
  0
);
const blackSum = myList.reduce(
  (result, v) => result + v.get('black'),
  0
);

console.log('myList', myList.toJS());
// -> myList [ { red: 3, black: 4 },
// ->          { red: 6, black: 8 },
// ->          { red: 9, black: 12 } ]
console.log('redSum', redSum);
// -> redSum 18
console.log('blackSum', blackSum);
// -> blackSum 24
```

The iteratee functions that we're using with `reduce()` are adding the `red` and `black` key values to the result, which then becomes the new result. We have two results here—`redSum` and `blackSum`—because we've made two calls to `reduce()`. Let's see if we can improve upon this:

```
const groupedSums = myList
  .reduce((result, v) => result
    .update('red', r => r + v.get('red'))
    .update('black', b => b + v.get('black'))
  );

console.log('groupedSums.red', groupedSums.get('red'));
// -> groupedSums.red 18
console.log('groupedSums.black', groupedSums.get('black'));
// -> groupedSums.black 24
```

Instead of implementing two `reduce()` calls to compute the two totals, we've now combined them into a single `reduce()` call. When you don't specify an initial reduction value, the first value of the collection is used. This means that you can call `update()` to increment the `red` and `black` keys and return the new map. The end result is a map where the `red` and `black` keys have the totals that you need.

Lazy mapping

The mapping that we've done so far has been called directly on collections. Mapping operations can be done lazily as part of a sequence of transformations that feed into a side-effect. Being able to filter and map lazily is part of a pattern that you'll use frequently with Immutable.js.

Multiple map() calls

Let's revisit our earlier example where we transformed two map values into a single capitalized name string:

```
const capitalize = s =>
  `${s.charAt(0).toUpperCase()}${s.slice(1)}`;
const myList = List.of(
  Map.of('first', 'joe', 'last', 'brown', 'age', 45),
  Map.of('first', 'john', 'last', 'smith', 'age', 32),
  Map.of('first', 'mary', 'last', 'wise', 'age', 56)
);
```

```
myList
  .toSeq()
  .map(v => v.update('first', capitalize))
  .map(v => v.update('last', capitalize))
  .map(v => [v.get('first'), v.get('last')].join(' '))
  .forEach(v => console.log('name', v));
  // -> name Joe Brown
  // -> name John Smith
  // -> name Mary Wise
```

In this version of the example, we're using sequences and side-effects to render the names. Once your list is converted to a sequence, you can call map() as many times as you like without creating new collections. Remember, values pass through sequence operations one at a time.

The first map() call updates the first key using the capitalize() function. The second map() call does the same thing, except with the last key. The final map() call before the side-effect joins the two key values together to form the resulting string.

Filtering before mapping

Let's modify our example slightly, building on this lazy mapping pattern. It's common to filter collections before mapping them so that they only include relevant values:

```
myList
  .toSeq()
  .filter(v => v.get('age') > 35)
  .map(v => v.update('first', capitalize))
  .map(v => v.update('last', capitalize))
  .map(v => [v.get('first'), v.get('last')].join(' '))
  .forEach(v => console.log('name', v));
  // -> name Joe Brown
  // -> name Mary Wise
```

In this case, we only want capitalized names where age is over 35. Once a filter match is found, it flows through each of the map() calls.

 When in doubt about how your sequence is lazily evaluating values, add logging to your iteratee and predicate functions so that you can see the order in which things are called. Stepping through the sequence using a debugger works too, if that's what you're more accustomed to.

The ultimate lazy pattern

This brings us to our ultimate lazy pattern. On their own, `filter()` and `map()` are powerful tools. You can add `reduce()` to the sequence as well, despite the fact that it isn't lazy. However, this doesn't stop the `map()` and `filter()` calls from executing lazily:

```
const capitalize = s =>
  `${s.charAt(0).toUpperCase()}${s.slice(1)}`;
const pick = (m, ...props) =>
  props.map(p => m.get(p));
const myList = List.of(
  Map.of('first', 'joe', 'last', 'brown', 'age', 45),
  Map.of('first', 'john', 'last', 'smith', 'age', 32),
  Map.of('first', 'mary', 'last', 'wise', 'age', 56)
);

console.log('myList', myList.toJS());
// -> myList [ { first: 'joe', last: 'brown', age: 45 },
// -> { first: 'john', last: 'smith', age: 32 },
// -> { first: 'mary', last: 'wise', age: 56 } ]

myList
  .toSeq()
  .filter(v => v.get('age') < 50)
  .map(v => v.update('first', capitalize))
  .map(v => v.update('last', capitalize))
  .map(v => v.set('name', pick(v, 'first', 'last').join(' ')))
  .reduce(
    (result, v) => result
      .update('age', a => a + v.get('age'))
      .update('names', n => n.push(v.get('name'))),
    Map.of('names', List(), 'age', 0)
  )
  .forEach(
    (v, k) => console.log(k, List.isList(v) ? v.toJS() : v)
  );
// -> names [ 'Joe Brown', 'John Smith' ]
// -> age 77
```

This example pulls together several things that we've looked at in this chapter. The end result is a reduction that is processed by a side-effect—a map with a list of names and the accumulated age of those names. What's interesting about Immutable.js sequences is that they still know how to perform lazy evaluation, even when you're using a method such as `reduce()` that doesn't support it.

Since `reduce()` needs to iterate over the entire collection that it is processing, it asks the sequence for one value at a time. It doesn't actually process the value, because it can't. But the lazy mapping and filtering still works as you would expect it, which is great news because it means that you don't have to allocate intermediary collections in between transformations.

This pattern also serves as an example of why method chaining is important. There are three aspects to this pattern: filtering, mapping, and reducing. Any of these are optional, and with the way that we've set up these method call chains, it's straightforward to add or remove any of these.

Summary

In this chapter, we looked at mapping and reducing Immutable.js collections, starting with producing simple values. We then looked at mapping lists of maps to new lists of maps, adding or removing keys along the way. Reducing collections means iterating over them and producing a value. If you can filter or map the collection instead, this should be the preferred approach.

Lazy evaluation is central to transforming Immutable.js collections before passing them to side-effects. We looked at how `map()` fits into lazy workflows and how it forms a common pattern for your applications in conjunction with `filter()` and `reduce()`.

In the next chapter, we'll look at some more advanced techniques for mapping and reducing collections.

8
Zipping and Flattening

Most transformations that you will perform on Immutable.js are some sort of map or reduce. For example, plucking key values from a list of maps is a mapping operation, while filtering collections is a reducing operation. In this chapter, we'll learn the following mapping and reducing techniques:

- Zipping collections
- Flattening collections

Zipping collections

You can iterate over more than one collection at the same time. This is what it means to **zip** collections together. By doing so, you can remove excessive iterations from your code. You can zip simple values and lists of maps, and you can lazy zip collections.

Removing excess iterations

When you're working with large collections, iterating over them can be expensive, especially when there are several of them to iterate over. Sometimes this can't be avoided. For example, a value in one list might depend on a value in a few other lists in the same index. Rather than structure your code so that it requires several iterations, the `zip()` method can remove these excess iterations.

Instead of having multiple mappers or iteratee functions, you can tell the collection that several other collections are required as arguments passed to a single iteratee. This means that you have to be aware of the order in which lists are zipped.

Zipping lists of simple values

Imagine that you have three separate sources of information for one logical entity. For example, you have the following:

- A list of names
- A list of roles
- A list of ages

The glue between these lists is their indexes. Using the `zip()` method, you can bring the values of these lists together, as follows:

```
const names = List.of('Jeremy', 'Garry', 'Katie');
const roles = List.of('Engineer', 'Designer', 'Programmer');
const ages = List.of(34, 23, 36);

names
  .zip(roles, ages)
  .map(v => v.join(', '))
  .forEach(v => console.log('employee', v));
// -> employee Jeremy, Engineer, 34
// -> employee Garry, Designer, 23
// -> employee Katie, Programmer, 36
```

The `names` list uses the `zip()` method to join the `roles` and `ages` lists together. The parameter that's passed to the `map()` iteratee is an array containing the values from all three lists. Our iteratee is returning the result of joining them all together as a single string, before passing it to the side-effect.

Zipping lists of maps

Since you don't always have a list of simple values with which to work, you need a way to zip more complex values together. If you're trying to zip lists of maps together, you probably don't want an array of maps passed to the next method in the chain. Using the `zipWith()` method, you can explicitly transform the zipped value using an iteratee that you provide, as shown here:

```
const names = List.of(
  Map.of('name', 'Jeremy'),
  Map.of('name', 'Garry'),
  Map.of('name', 'Katie')
);
const roles = List.of(
  Map.of('role', 'Engineer'),
```

```
  Map.of('role', 'Designer'),
  Map.of('role', 'Programmer')
);
const ages = List.of(
  Map.of('age', 34),
  Map.of('age', 23),
  Map.of('age', 36)
);

names
  .zipWith(
    (...colls) => Map().merge(...colls),
    roles,
    ages
  )
  .forEach(v => console.log('employee', v.toJS()));
  // -> employee { name: 'Jeremy', role: 'Engineer', age: 34 }
  // -> employee { name: 'Garry', role: 'Designer', age: 23 }
  // -> employee { name: 'Katie', role: 'Programmer', age: 36 }
```

The first argument to `zipWith()` is the iteratee function. Since you know that you're dealing with lists of maps in this example, you can call `merge()`, passing to it the `colls` array. This results in a single map, as shown in the side-effect output.

Lazy zipping

The zipping methods that we've looked at so far have all been called on lists. If you want to lazily zip lists together, you have to use a sequence, as follows:

```
names
  .toSeq()
  .zipWith(
    (...maps) => Map().merge(...maps),
    roles,
    ages
  )
  .forEach(v => console.log('lazy zipWith', v.toJS()));
  // -> lazy zipWith { name: 'Jeremy', role: 'Engineer', age: 34 }
  // -> lazy zipWith { name: 'Garry', role: 'Designer', age: 23 }
  // -> lazy zipWith { name: 'Katie', role: 'Programmer', age: 36 }
```

You don't have to convert each of your lists to sequences in order to lazy zip them together. By calling `toSeq()` on the `names` list just before calling `zipWith()`, you're zipping together one map at a time as it's fed into the `forEach()` side-effect. Now that we're using a sequence for lazy zipping, let's look at another approach:

```
names
  .toSeq()
  .zip(roles, ages)
  .map(maps => Map().merge(...maps))
  .forEach(v => console.log('lazy zip', v.toJS()));
// -> lazy zip { name: 'Jeremy', role: 'Engineer', age: 34 }
// -> lazy zip { name: 'Garry', role: 'Designer', age: 23 }
// -> lazy zip { name: 'Katie', role: 'Programmer', age: 36 }
```

Instead of using `zipWith()` we'll be using `zip()`, which results in an array of maps being passed to the next method. Then, we use `map()` to perform our merge. This approach is very similar to `zipWith()`—since we're now using a sequence to execute things lazily, there's no harm in putting our map merging logic into a separate `map()` call. Remember, sequences don't create new collections in between chained method calls.

Flattening collections

Collections in Immutable.js can have simple values, or they can have complex values such as other collections. These collections can in turn contain other collections, and so on. These deep structures are necessary to reflect the model of your application data. However, traversing nested hierarchies is error prone.

Avoiding recursion

When you're dealing with hierarchical data, recursion is inevitable. We write a function that calls itself when a new level in the hierarchy is discovered. This is difficult to do because these types of functions often end up being highly specialized, applying to only one situation. With Immutable.js and its persistent-change/transformation/side-effect pattern, writing recursive functions is often a dead end.

When traversing nested collections, you don't often care where you are in the hierarchy. So, if all you need is to locate a particular value, it's much simpler to traverse a flat collection.

 The downside to flattening collections is that you have to iterate over the entire nested structure before you can use the flat list. The positive tradeoff is that the flat collection is cheaper to process.

Deep flattening nested lists

By default, Immutable.js will **deep flatten** collections. This means that it will recursively traverse nested collections to an arbitrary depth, adding values to a flat collection. Let's flatten a nested list structure and filter the resulting collection:

```
import { fromJS } from 'immutable';

const myList = fromJS([
  [1, 2],
  [3, 4],
  [
    [5, 6],
    [
      [7, 8],
      [9, 10],
      [
        [11, 12],
        [13, 14],
        [
          [15, 16],
          [17, 18],
          [
            [19, 20]
          ]
        ]
      ]
    ]
  ]
]);

console.log('myList', myList.flatten().toJS());
// -> myList [ 1, 2, 3, 4, 5, 6, 7, 8, 9, 10,
// -> 11, 12, 13, 14, 15, 16, 17, 18,
// -> 19, 20 ]

// We're looking for odd numbers in a deeply-nested
```

```
// list of numbers. If we convert the list to a sequence,
// then flatten it, we can avoid recursion, and flatten
// the list lazily.
myList
  .toSeq()
  .flatten()
  .filter(v => v % 2)
  .take(5)
  .forEach(v => console.log('odd', v));
// -> odd 1
// -> odd 3
// -> odd 5
// -> odd 7
// -> odd 9
```

Here, we're converting this list into a sequence before flattening it so that we can lazily iterate over the filtered results. We're only taking five values from the sequence (`take(5)`), which means that the `flatten()` method only needs to traverse this deeply-nested structure until it finds five values that pass the `filter()` predicate.

Shallow flattening lists

Sometimes, you don't want the default behavior of `flatten()`, which is to deep flatten collections. Instead, you want to shallow flatten the collection. For example, if you know the structure of the data with which you are dealing, you might not want to include deeply-nested collection values in the flattened result:

```
const myList = List.of(
  List.of('first', 'second'),
  List.of('third', 'fourth', List.of('fifth')),
  List.of('sixth', 'seventh')
);
const myFlattenedList = myList.flatten();
const myShallowList = myList
  .flatten(true)
  .filterNot(List.isList);

console.log('myList', myList.toJS());
// -> myList [ [ 'first', 'second' ],
// ->          [ 'third', 'fourth', [ 'fifth' ] ],
// ->          [ 'sixth', 'seventh' ] ]

console.log('myFlattenedList', myFlattenedList.toJS());
// -> myFlattenedList [ 'first', 'second', 'third', 'fourth',
// ->                   'fifth', 'sixth', 'seventh' ]
```

```
console.log('myShallowList', myShallowList.toJS());
// -> myShallowList [ 'first', 'second', 'third', 'fourth',
// ->                   'sixth', 'seventh' ]
```

By passing true to flatten(), it will only go one level deep when looking for nested collections. There's a nested list in myList. You can see that myFlattenedList was created by calling flatten() and that it contains fifth. This could be a problem if your code expects lists beyond the first level to stay as lists. When you call flatten(true) to shallow flatten myList, you can simply remove the list values from the flattened result.

Flattening nested maps

Another common structure is deeply-nested maps. Let's imagine that you want to filter keys, including nested keys, by flattening the nested map structure:

```
const myMap = Map.of(
  'first', 1,
  'second', Map.of(
    'third', 3,
    'fourth', 4,
    'fifth', Map.of(
      'sixth', Map.of(
        'seventh', 7
      )
    )
  )
);

console.log('myMap', myMap.toJS());
// -> { first: 1,
// ->   second: {
// ->     third: 3,
// ->     fourth: 4,
// ->     fifth: {
// ->       sixth: { seventh: 7 } } } }

myMap
  .toSeq()
  .flatten()
  .filter((v, k) => k.startsWith('f'))
  .forEach((v, k) => console.log(k, v));
// -> first 1
// -> fourth 4
```

Here, we are able to find all nested values whose key started with ' f '. One of the keys—' fifth '—starts with ' f ', but it doesn't appear in the results. When you flatten maps, the flattened sequence doesn't include keys whose values are collections.

Summary

In this chapter, you learned about zipping and flattening collections. You zip collections together when you want to avoid having to iterate over several collections. Instead, you pass data from each collection to the iteratee function. Flattening collections is done to avoid having to traverse nested collections recursively when looking for a value. It's much easier to have the flatten() method do this for us and then iterate over a flat collection.

In the next chapter, we'll look at detecting whether or not collections have actually changed.

9
Persistent Change Detection

Immutable.js collections can never change. Instead, they have methods that implement **persistent changes**; that is, they return a new collection with the expected change in it. In this chapter, we'll explore how to detect changes in collections. In particular, you'll learn about the following:

- Performing strict collection equality comparisons
- The difference between strict equality and deep equality
- The difference between transformations and mutations
- Caching parameters and side-effects

Collection equality

There are two types of equality checks that you can use with Immutable.js collections: strict equality and deep equality. Strict equality is cheaper and therefore it is faster than deep equality. On the other hand, there are some things that deep equality can do that strict equality cannot.

Strict equality and mutative methods

In JavaScript, the strict equality operator compares the memory address of values, not the actual values. Immutable.js collections can't be changed, which means that the strict equality operator doesn't make much sense to use with Immutable.js collections. There's one important use case where this operator does make sense to use with Immutable.js collections—change detection.

Detecting changes

What's special about **mutative methods**, or methods that perform persistent changes, is that they return the same collection instance if nothing actually changes. This is a big deal because it means that you can use strict equality to detect a change in the collection, as shown here:

```
const myList = List.of(1, 2, 3);
const myMap = Map.of(
  'one', 1,
  'two', 2,
  'three', 3
);
const myModifiedList = myList.push(4);
const myModifiedMap = myMap.set('four', 4);

console.log('myList', myList.toJS());
// -> myList [ 1, 2, 3 ]
console.log('myMap', myMap.toJS());
// -> myMap { one: 1, two: 2, three: 3 }
console.log('myModifiedList', myModifiedList.toJS());
// -> myModifiedList [ 1, 2, 3, 4 ]
console.log('myModifiedMap', myModifiedMap.toJS());
// -> myModifiedMap { one: 1, two: 2, three: 3, four: 4 }
console.log(
  'myList === myModifiedList',
  myList === myModifiedList
);
// -> myList === myModifiedList false
console.log(
  'myMap === myModifiedMap',
  myMap === myModifiedMap
);
// -> myMap === myModifiedMap false
```

We have two initial collections in this example: `myList` and `myMap`. We then proceed to call mutative methods on these collections and store the results. The list gets a new value via the `push()` method and the map gets a new key-value pair via the `set()` method. When you compare the initial collections with their corresponding changed collections, you can see that they're not equal—the strict equality operator returns `false` in both instances. This is the expected behavior, because we changed the collections by adding new values.

Detecting no changes

The same methods that we used in the previous example will return the same collection instance if nothing has changed. Why shouldn't they? Allocating a new instance would be wasting resources. Additionally, we can use the highly efficient strict equality operator to check for changes. We know that when two collections are equal, nothing has changed:

```
const myUnmodifiedList = myList.set(0, 1);
const myUnmodifiedMap = myMap.set('one', 1);

console.log('myUnmodifiedList', myUnmodifiedList.toJS());
// -> myUnmodifiedList [ 1, 2, 3 ]
console.log('myUnmodifiedMap', myUnmodifiedMap.toJS());
// -> myUnmodifiedMap { one: 1, two: 2, three: 3 }
console.log(
  'myList === myUnmodifiedList',
  myList === myUnmodifiedList
);
// -> myList === myUnmodifiedList true
console.log(
  'myMap === myUnmodifiedMap',
  myMap === myUnmodifiedMap
);
// -> myMap === myUnmodifiedMap true
```

The set() method calls used in this example don't result in any values changing. We're setting the first list value to its current value and we're setting the 'one' map value to its current value. This results in the same collection being returned and the strict equality operator evaluating to true. We now have a reliable approach to change detection with collections since mutative methods will always return the same instance if it can.

Strict equality versus deep equality

Strict equality has limited utility compared to deep equality. Strict equality is great for efficiently checking if a collection has changed after calling a mutative method. In fact, you can use either strict equality or deep equality to check if a collection has changed:

```
const myMap = Map.of('first', 1);
const myModifiedMap = myMap.set('first', 'first');
const myUnmodifiedMap = myMap.set('first', 1);

console.log('myMap', myMap.toJS());
// -> myMap { first: 1 }
console.log('myModifiedMap', myModifiedMap.toJS());
// -> myModifiedMap { first: 'first' }
```

```
console.log('myUnmodifiedMap', myUnmodifiedMap.toJS());
// -> myUnmodifiedMap { first: 1 }

console.log(
  'myMap === myModifiedMap',
  myMap === myModifiedMap
);
// -> myMap === myModifiedMap false
console.log(
  'myMap === myUnmodifiedMap',
  myMap === myUnmodifiedMap
);
// -> myMap === myUnmodifiedMap true
console.log(
  'myMap.equals(myModifiedMap)',
  myMap.equals(myModifiedMap)
);
// -> myMap.equals(myModifiedMap) false
console.log(
  'myMap.equals(myUnmodifiedMap)',
  myMap.equals(myUnmodifiedMap)
);
// -> myMap.equals(Map.of('first', 1)) true
```

Using `equals()` yields the result that you would expect. The downside is that it is a deep operation that has to do a lot of work to compare the two collections. Strict equality is fast because it only compares the collection references. The downside to strict equality is that it can be misused in certain contexts. For example, you could mistakenly use strict equality to compare collections:

```
console.log(
  'myMap.equals(Map.of(\'first\', 1))',
  myMap.equals(Map.of('first', 1))
);
// -> myMap.equals(Map.of('first', 1)) true
console.log(
  'myMap === Map.of(\'first\', 1)',
  myMap === Map.of('first', 1)
);
// -> myMap === Map.of('first', 1) false
```

In this context, we just want to check if the collections are equal (as opposed to checking if it changed). Strict equality fails here because the references are different. The `equals()` method gives the correct result because it's using deep equality to compare the collection values.

Transformations versus mutations

Transformation methods and mutative methods can be a source of confusion when it comes to change detection. **Transformation methods** are used to provide a side-effect with the data that it needs to detect changes. **Mutative methods** produce a new collection as a new version of the old collection.

Transformations always return new collections

Mutative methods will return the same collection reference if nothing actually changes. This is what enables strict equality change detection. Transformation methods, on the other hand, don't have this capability. This means that if a transformation method results in the exact same collection values, it still returns a new reference. Let's look at the difference between mutated collections and transformed collections:

```
const myList = List.of(
  Map.of('one', 1, 'two', 2),
  Map.of('three', 3, 'four', 4),
  Map.of('five', 5, 'six', 6)
);
const myTransformedList = myList.map(v => v);
const myMutatedList = myList
  .update(0, v => v.set('one', 1));

console.log('myList', myList.toJS());
// -> myList [ { one: 1, two: 2 },
// ->          { three: 3, four: 4 },
// ->          { five: 5, six: 6 } ]
console.log('myTransformedList', myTransformedList.toJS());
// -> myTransformedList [ { one: 1, two: 2 },
// ->                     { three: 3, four: 4 },
// ->                     { five: 5, six: 6 } ]
console.log('myMutatedList', myMutatedList.toJS());
// -> myMutatedList [ { one: 1, two: 2 },
// ->                 { three: 3, four: 4 },
// ->                 { five: 5, six: 6 } ]
console.log(
```

```
  'myList === myTransformedList',
  myList === myTransformedList
);
// -> myList === myTransformedList false
console.log(
  'myList === myMutatedList',
  myList === myMutatedList
);
// -> myList === myMutatedList true
```

All three of these collections—myList, myTransformedList, and myMutatedList—have identical values. When you compare myList to myTransformedList using strict equality, they don't match. This is because myTransformedList was created using map(), which is a transformation method. On the other hand, myList and myMutatedList do match when compared using strict equality. This is because update() is mutative.

If you want to compare transformed lists with their originals, you should use the equals() method:

```
console.log(
  'myList.equals(myTransformedList)',
  myList.equals(myTransformedList)
);
// -> myList.equals(myTransformedList) true
console.log(
  'myList.equals(myMutatedList)',
  myList.equals(myMutatedList)
);
// -> myList.equals(myMutatedList) true
```

This will yield consistent results, no matter how the collection was created.

Detecting changes before transformations

With Immutable.js collections, the idea is to detect any changes before any transformations and side-effects are run. You could, for example, detect changes after transformations but before side-effects:

```
const myList = List.of(1, 2, 3);
const mySideEffect = (list) => {
  const transformed = list
    .map(v => v * v);

  if (!transformed.equals(mySideEffect.prev)) {
    mySideEffect.prev = transformed;
```

```
    transformed.forEach(
      v => console.log('transformed', v)
    );
  }
};

mySideEffect(myList);
// -> transformed 1
// -> transformed 4
// -> transformed 9
mySideEffect(myList.set(0, 1));
mySideEffect(myList.push(4));
// -> transformed 1
// -> transformed 4
// -> transformed 9
// -> transformed 16
mySideEffect(myList.push(4));
```

The `mySideEffect()` function transforms a list of numbers and then iterates over the results, logging the values. The second and fourth calls to `mySideEffect()` don't log any values, because we're passing in the same value that was used in the previous call. These values are stored in the `prev` property of the function, and if the `list` argument is the same collection, we skip the side-effect.

 Skipping side-effects is useful because it means that you don't have to perform expensive operations such as updating DOM nodes or writing to a file.

The problem with this approach is that we're comparing the result of the transformation with a previous transformation result. You don't need to do this. Instead, you should only compare the collection argument itself:

```
const myList = List.of(1, 2, 3);
const myModifiedList = myList.push(4);

const mySideEffect = (list) => {
  if (list !== mySideEffect.prev) {
    mySideEffect.prev = list;
    list
      .map(v => v * v)
      .forEach(v => console.log('transformed', v));
  }
};

mySideEffect(myList);
// -> transformed 1
```

```
// -> transformed 4
// -> transformed 9
mySideEffect(myList.set(0, 1));
mySideEffect(myModifiedList);
// -> transformed 1
// -> transformed 4
// -> transformed 9
// -> transformed 16
mySideEffect(myModifiedList.set(0, 1));
```

We've introduced two improvements to `mySideEffect()` here. First, we're detecting changes to the collection before any transformations are run. This could potentially save a lot of computing effort. Second, since we're detecting changes before transformations happen, we only care about mutative methods, which means that we can compare using strict inequality instead of `equals()`. This is another potential performance improvement.

One downside to `mySideEffect()` is that it's not a generic solution. Your application will likely have several side-effects. Another downside is that your side-effect functions could need more than a single collection argument in order to transform data needed by the side-effect.

Caching side-effects

By detecting that no changes have been made in a collection, you can skip the side-effect that would otherwise iterate over the collection, possibly running transformations along the way. Essentially, you're caching the side-effect. Usually, when you cache functions, you cache a value that's returned by the function. Side-effects are different because they effect the external environment in some way. For example, a UI component that uses an Immutable.js collection has been rendered. You then ask the component to render itself again, even though the collection that it uses hasn't changed at all. This side-effect can simply be ignored since it's already represented by the UI.

Let's build a generic mechanism that can be used to cache arbitrary side-effect functions:

```
const sideEffectCache = new WeakMap();
const sideEffect = fn => (...args) => {
  const cache = sideEffectCache.get(fn)
    || new Array(args.length);
  const miss = Seq(args)
    .zip(cache)
    .some(([a, b]) => a !== b);

  if (miss) {
    sideEffectCache.set(fn, args);
    fn(...args);
  }
};
```

We've created a `WeakMap` instance, `sideEffectCache`, to store functions and the last set of arguments with which it was called. The `sideEffect()` function takes a function argument—the actual side-effect to run—and returns a new function. The returned function will check `sideEffectCache` to see if it's being called with the exact same collection arguments as the last time. Using strict inequality to compare each `args` value to it's corresponding cache value, we determine whether or not the function call is the same as the last one. If it's the same, then we don't have to run the side-effect at all. If it's not the same, then we update the cache and run the side-effect.

Let's compose some side-effect functions as follows:

```
const renderOddNumbers = sideEffect(
  coll => coll
    .toSeq()
    .filterNot(v => v % 2)
    .take(5)
    .forEach(v => console.log('odd', v))
);
const renderMultiples = sideEffect(
  (a, b) => a
    .toSeq()
    .zip(b)
    .map(([v1, v2]) => v1 * v2)
    .take(5)
    .forEach(v => console.log('multiple', v))
);
```

Both of these side-effect functions perform a bunch of transformations before ending with a `forEach()` side-effect iteration that logs values. The `renderOddNumbers()` function has only one argument to cache while the `renderMultiples()` function has two arguments that can impact its side-effect. Let's give these two functions an initial run:

```
const myFirstList = List.of(
  1, 2, 3, 4, 5, 6, 7, 8, 9, 10,
  11, 12, 13, 14, 15, 16, 17, 18, 19, 20
);
const mySecondList = List.of(
  21, 22, 23, 24, 25, 26, 27, 28, 29, 30,
  31, 32, 33, 34, 35, 36, 37, 38, 39, 40
);

console.log('first render');
renderOddNumbers(myFirstList);
renderMultiples(myFirstList, mySecondList);
// -> first render
// -> odd 2
// -> odd 4
// -> odd 6
// -> odd 8
// -> odd 10
// -> multiple 21
// -> multiple 44
// -> multiple 69
// -> multiple 96
// -> multiple 125
```

As expected, both side-effects run because they haven't been run at all yet. Let's try this again with some new argument values:

```
console.log('second render');
renderOddNumbers(myFirstList.set(0, 1));
renderMultiples(myFirstList, mySecondList.set(0, 21));
// -> second render
```

The side-effects didn't run, because we're calling `set()` in such a way that the same collection reference is returned. This means that the collections are found in the cache by `sideEffect()`, and the side-effect isn't run because it doesn't need to.

Let's run these side-effects one more time with data that's actually changed:

```
console.log('third render');
renderOddNumbers(myFirstList.insert(0, -1));
renderMultiples(
  myFirstList,
  mySecondList.push(100)
);
// -> third render
// -> odd 2
// -> odd 4
// -> odd 6
// -> odd 8
// -> odd 10
// -> multiple 21
// -> multiple 44
// -> multiple 69
// -> multiple 96
// -> multiple 125
```

Both of the side-effects are run because the collections that are passed as arguments aren't found in `sideEffectCache`. With the `sideEffect()` utility in place, you now have a means to cache side-effects by caching the last set of arguments with which it was called.

Summary

In this chapter, we looked at change detection with Immutable.js collections. The main objective with change detection is avoiding side-effects when the data is the same as it was the last time the side-effect ran. We looked at using strict equality to compare collections. This works because mutative methods return the same reference when nothing has changed. Using strict equality as the mechanism for change detection can have a dramatic impact on overall application performance. For any other collection comparisons, you want to use deep equality with the `equals()` method.

We then implemented change detection that avoided running side-effects when the input collections didn't change from the first time the side-effect ran. We turned this into a generic function that can produce functions that have built-in side-effect caching abilities.

In the next chapter, you'll learn about sets—collections with unique values.

10
Working with Sets

Immutable.js sets are used to store unique values. Some libraries have functions or methods to remove duplicate values from lists or arrays. If you want to remove duplicate values from Immutable.js lists, the solution is to convert the collection code into a set. In this chapter, you'll learn do the following:

- See that sets aren't a substitute for lists
- Remove duplicates from lists by converting them to sets
- Use ordered sets to sort sets and iterate over them
- Maintain sets by adding unique values and preventing duplicates from being added

Sets are not lists

At the first glance, sets look a lot like lists. There are a number of important differences to keep in mind, however. The most important thing to remember is that sets are not an indexed collection like lists, meaning that you can't rely on the iteration order, nor can you look up values by index. **Sets** are a special type of collection whose main use is in removing duplicate values.

Do not use the get() method

Sets have a `get()` method because it's inherited from the base `Collection` class. The `get()` method looks for values by index for lists and by key for maps. Sets are interesting, because they have neither indexes nor keys. So, despite the fact that sets have a `get()` method, it probably doesn't do what you think it does. Take a look at the following code:

```
const myList = List.of(1, 2, 3);
const mySet = Set.of(1, 2, 3);

console.log('myList', myList.toJS());
// -> myList [ 1, 2, 3 ]
console.log('mySet', mySet.toJS());
// -> mySet [ 1, 2, 3 ]

// Using get() with sets as though they're indexed
// collections doesn't work.
console.log('myList.get(0)', myList.get(0));
// -> myList.get(0) 1
console.log('mySet.get(0)', mySet.get(0));
// -> mySet.get(0) undefined
```

As you can see, when we try to get the first item of the set, as we would do with a list, we don't get the expected value. Again, this is because sets aren't indexed collections; so don't use `get()`.

No defined iteration order

Sets are like maps in that they don't have a defined iteration order. This means that using a `for...of` loop or the `forEach()` method could have unexpected results, as follows:

```
console.log('myList.forEach()');
myList.forEach(v => console.log(v));
// -> myList.forEach()
// -> 1
// -> 2
// -> 3
console.log('mySet.forEach()');
mySet.forEach(v => console.log(v));
// -> mySet.forEach()
// -> 1
// -> 2
// -> 3
```

When a collection isn't indexed numerically, don't count on consistent iteration behavior. You could end up seeing consistent iteration behavior in one JavaScript engine and a different behavior in another. The iteration behavior of sets is stable, meaning that the order doesn't change once it's already been iterated over, but this doesn't matter if we can't predict the order in different environments.

Maps with keys only

Under the hood, sets are maps with no values. When a value is added to a set, it's added to an internal map as a key. It also adds a value because it has to do so, but it isn't used for anything. This is done so that Immutable.js can reuse the map implementation for the purpose of removing duplicate values using deep equality. For example, if you were to add a key to a map and this key was already set, it isn't going to add another version of the same key. It will just update the value.

This internal detail explains why the get() method doesn't work the way you might think that it should, and why set iteration behaves the same way as map iteration.

Removing duplicates

Sets aren't usually created directly. Instead, you convert lists of values that might have duplicates into sets to remove the duplicates.

Converting to sets

Assuming that you have a list that might contain duplicate values, you can convert the list to a set, as follows:

```
const myList = List.of(1, 1, 2, 2, 3, 3);
const mySet = myList.toSet();

console.log('myList', myList.toJS());
// -> myList [ 1, 1, 2, 2, 3, 3 ]
console.log('mySet', mySet.toJS());
// -> mySet [ 1, 2, 3 ]
```

As you can see, mySet has unique values from myList. The problem now is that you need to be able to use these unique values as part of an indexed collection. In other words, you need to convert the set back into a list.

Converting to sets, then back to lists

Once we've converted our list to a set, we'll have removed any duplicates. However, we do useful things with lists, such as getting values at a specific index or iterating over values in a consistent order. To do this, we'll convert our set back to a list, as shown here:

```
const myUniqueList = myList
  .toSet()
  .toList();

console.log('myUniqueList', myUniqueList.toJS());
// -> myUniqueList [ 1, 2, 3 ]
```

Using this approach, the set is an intermediary collection. Using sets ephemerally to enforce uniqueness is a common pattern in Immutable.js applications.

Lazy duplicate removal

What if you have large collections in your application? The ability to execute lazily is key to Immutable.js being able to scale. Using sets to lazily remove duplicates from a collection isn't so simple. Let's give it a shot:

```
const myList = List.of(
  Map.of('one', 1, 'two', 2),
  Map.of('three', 3, 'four', 4),
  Map.of('one', 1, 'two', 2),
  Map.of('five', 5, 'six', 6),
  Map.of('one', 1, 'two', 2)
);

myList
  .toSetSeq()
  .map(v => v.toJS())
  .forEach(v => console.log('toSetSeq()', v));
// -> toSetSeq() { one: 1, two: 2 }
// -> toSetSeq() { three: 3, four: 4 }
// -> toSetSeq() { one: 1, two: 2 }
// -> toSetSeq() { five: 5, six: 6 }
// -> toSetSeq() { one: 1, two: 2 }
```

This didn't work as expected. We used `toSetSeq()` to convert `myList` into a set sequence. Unfortunately, this doesn't actually remove duplicates. The reason that we're trying to convert this list into a sequence is so that we can perform our `forEach()` side-effect lazily. However, because this is a lazy sequence, it's not able to remove duplicates.

The `toSetSeq()` method is misleading and should be avoided. Let's try another approach:

```
myList
  .toSet()
  .toSeq()
  .map(v => v.toJS())
  .forEach(v => console.log('toSet()', v));
// -> toSet() { one: 1, two: 2 }
// -> toSet() { three: 3, four: 4 }
// -> toSet() { five: 5, six: 6 }
```

This produces the expected result, but not everything is performed lazily. We have to convert `myList` to a set and then to a sequence. This means that the `map()` and `forEach()` calls are done lazily; however, when we convert the list to a set using `toSet()`, we have to iterate over the whole collection up front. You don't want to iterate over entire collections.

Let's try one more approach:

```
const lazySet = (list) => {
  let seen = Set();

  return list
    .toSeq()
    .filter((v) => {
      if (seen.includes(v)) {
        return false;
      }

      seen = seen.add(v);
      return true;
    });
};
const myBigList = myList.concat(
  Repeat(Map.of('one', 1, 'two', 2), 10000)
);

console.log('myBigList.size', myBigList.size);
// -> myBigList.size 10005
lazySet(myBigList)
  .map(v => v.toJS())
  .take(2)
  .forEach(v => console.log('lazySet()', v));
// -> lazySet() { one: 1, two: 2 }
// -> lazySet() { three: 3, four: 4 }
```

This delivers the expected result because we're doing it lazily. The `lazySet()` function uses `filter()` to remove duplicates instead of using a `Set` type. It keeps values that have already made it through in a `seen` set. We then use this set to check if any values have already been returned. If there were any, we know it's a duplicate and ignore it.

We're adding `10,000` duplicate values to `myList` in this example to illustrate the savings of this approach. Since we're using `filter()` to remove duplicates, this can be done lazily. We're using `take()` to say that we only want 2 values. There are only three unique values in the collection, but since we're removing duplicates lazily, we don't have to iterate over the collection `10,000` times. We've capped the maximum number of iterations at 2.

You might have noticed that we've found a new use for sets in the `lazySet()` function. The `seen` variable is a `Set` collection because we only need it to store unique values, and we don't need to iterate over it. We only need to check for the existence of a value. So, if you find yourself in a scenario where you need to hold on to unique values temporarily in order to check if one of them is a specific value, sets are a good choice.

Ordered sets

When you convert sets to lists, you run the risk of adding values to the list out of order. Sets have no defined order, because they're not indexed collections. Immutable.js has an `OrderedSet` collection type that acts like an `OrderedMap`. It preserves the insertion order of its values. Other than that, it is just like a regular set.

Internally, `Set` uses `Map` to store its values as map keys. `OrderedSet` uses the `OrderedMap` keys.

Sorting sets

You can use ordered sets to remove duplicate values and maintain the value insertion order. This means that you can do things such as converting a list to an ordered set, sorting the set, and then converting it back to a list. Examine the following:

```
const myList = List.of(
  1, 3, 1, 2, 3, 4, 1, 5,
  2, 4, 6, 1, 5, 2, 7, 1,
  8, 3, 7, 1, 4, 2, 8, 9
```

```
);
const myUniqueList = myList
  .toOrderedSet()
  .sort()
  .reverse()
  .toList();

console.log('myList', myList.toJS());
// -> myList [ 1, 3, 1, 2, 3, 4, 1, 5, 2, 4, 6,
// ->          1, 5, 2, 7, 1, 8, 3, 7, 1, 4, 2,
// ->          8, 9 ]
console.log('myUniqueList', myUniqueList.toJS());
// -> myUniqueList [ 9, 8, 7, 6, 5,
// ->               4, 3, 2, 1 ]
```

The key here is that the list is converted to an ordered set before any sorting happens. Not only does this remove duplicate values, it also ensures that any changes that you make to the ordering of values will be preserved. This means that you can convert the ordered set into a list with confidence that the values will be in the correct order.

Iterating over sets

If you just want to remove duplicates before you iterate over the collection, you don't need to convert ordered sets back to lists. You can just iterate over the ordered set, as follows:

```
const myOrderedSet = myList
  .toOrderedSet()
  .sort()
  .reverse();

myOrderedSet.forEach(v => console.log('myOrderedSet', v));
// -> myOrderedSet 9
// -> myOrderedSet 8
// -> myOrderedSet 7
// -> myOrderedSet 6
// -> myOrderedSet 5
// -> myOrderedSet 4
// -> myOrderedSet 3
// -> myOrderedSet 2
// -> myOrderedSet 1
```

Our side-effect code can iterate over the set as if it were a list, without the fear of things being out of order.

Maintaining sets

Being able to remove duplicate values from lists is great. The problem with this approach is that you have to remove duplicates every time that you run a side-effect. This is wasteful for two reasons:

- You're storing values that aren't used for anything
- You have to spend valuable CPU cycles to get rid of them

To counter these issues, you can just use ordered sets instead of lists to prevent duplicates from ever appearing in the first place.

Adding unique values

Let's implement a function that prints set values only if the set argument value has changed since the last time it was called:

```
const printValues = (set) => {
  if (!set.equals(printValues.prev)) {
    printValues.prev = set;
    set
      .valueSeq()
      .map(v => v.toJS())
      .forEach(v => console.log(v));
  }
};
```

If this code looks familiar, it's because you learned about this change detection technique in the previous chapter. The reason that we need this here is so that we can see how sets change as we add values to them:

```
const myOrderedSet = OrderedSet.of(
  Map.of('one', 1),
  Map.of('two', 2)
);

console.log('myOrderedSet');
printValues(myOrderedSet);
// -> myOrderedSet
// -> { one: 1 }
// -> { two: 2 }
console.log('adding 3');
printValues(myOrderedSet.add(Map.of('three', 3)));
// -> adding 3
```

```
// -> { one: 1 }
// -> { two: 2 }
// -> { three: 3 }
```

The first call to printValues() prints everything in the collection because nothing has changed. The second call prints values too because we're adding a unique value to myOrderedSet.

Adding duplicate values

Let's see what happens when we call printValues() when we try adding a duplicate value to myOrderedSet:

```
console.log('adding 3 again');
printValues(myOrderedSet.add(Map.of('three', 3)));
// -> adding 3 again
```

The side-effect doesn't run because the value that we're trying to add with add() isn't actually added since it's a duplicate of a value that's already in the set.

Summary

This chapter introduced you to the Set collection of Immutable.js. The fundamental feature of sets is that they don't allow duplicate values. By converting lists to sets, you can remove duplicate values. If you try adding a duplicate value to a set, it just won't get added.

One challenge with sets is that they're not indexed, which means that you can't rely on consistent iteration behavior. The answer to this is to use ordered sets, which are capable of preserving the insertion order of values.

In the next chapter, you'll learn about comparing collections.

11
Comparing Collections

We can compare Immutable.js collections to determine their equality. Much of the time, collections aren't exactly equal. In this chapter, we'll utilize the functionality of Immutable.js to help us determine the degrees of equality and inequality of collections by doing the following:

- Finding the intersection of sets
- Intersection techniques
- Finding the difference between collections
- Map intersections and differences
- Finding supersets and subsets of lists

Set intersections

An **intersection** is part of two or more collections that are the same. Immutable.js sets have built-in capabilities for finding intersections.

Intersecting sets

Let's start by creating two sets:

```
const myFirstSet = Set.of(1, 2, 3, 4, 5, 6);
const mySecondSet = Set.of(2, 4, 6, 8, 10);
```

The intersection between these two sets are the values 2, 4, and 6—they exist in both collections. Sets have an `intersect()` method that will find this intersection for you, as follows:

```
const myIntersection = myFirstSet.intersect(mySecondSet);

console.log('myFirstSet', myFirstSet.toJS());
// -> myFirstSet [ 1, 2, 3, 4, 5, 6 ]
console.log('mySecondSet', mySecondSet.toJS());
// -> mySecondSet [ 2, 4, 6, 8, 10 ]
console.log('myIntersection', myIntersection.toJS());
// -> myIntersection [ 6, 2, 4 ]
```

The values in `myIntersection` look good, but they appear to be out of order. This is because the iteration order of sets isn't defined.

Ordered intersections

You can preserve the order of the first set by transforming it to an ordered set:

```
const myOrderedIntersection = myFirstSet
  .sort()
  .intersect(mySecondSet);

console.log('myOrderedIntersection', myOrderedIntersection.toJS());
// -> myOrderedIntersection [ 2, 4, 6 ]
```

This works because `myFirstSet` is now an ordered set. When you sort it, it returns an `OrderedSet` which remains sorted when the `intersect()` method iterates over it.

List intersections

Sets have an `intersect()` method because it's assumed that if you need to find the intersection of values, these values should be unique. This makes sense, but you don't have to convert your lists into sets just for the sake of finding intersecting values.

Reducing list intersections

You can intersect list values using the `reduce()` method. Let's create a function that will intersect the list values given to it:

```
const intersect = (...lists) => {
  const [head] = lists;
  const tail = Seq(lists.slice(1));

  return head.reduce((result, value) =>
    tail
      .map(list => list.includes(value))
      .includes(false) ?
        result : result.add(value),
    Set()
  );
};
```

The `intersect()` function accepts an arbitrary number of lists, using the rest parameter syntax (`...`). The first step is to get the **head** and **tail** of these lists. The `head` constant represents the first list while the `tail` constant represents the remaining lists.

We'll use `head` as the list to iterate over using `reduce()`. Within `reduce()`, we map `tail` to see if any of these lists contain the current value using `includes()`. Now we have a list of Boolean values. If any of them are `false`, this means that the value isn't in every list that was passed to `intersect()`, and we don't include it in the reduction.

As you can see, we're using `Set` as the reduced intersection to prevent duplicate values. Let's see what the results look like:

```
const myList1 = List.of(1, 2, 3, 2);
const myList2 = List.of(2, 3, 4);
const myList3 = List.of(2, 3, 5);
const myIntersection = intersect(
  myList1,
  myList2,
  myList3
);

console.log('myList1', myList1.toJS());
// -> myList1 [ 1, 2, 3, 2 ]
console.log('myList2', myList2.toJS());
// -> myList2 [ 2, 3, 4 ]
console.log('myList3', myList3.toJS());
// -> myList3 [ 2, 3, 5 ]
console.log('myIntersection', myIntersection.toJS());
```

```
// -> myIntersection [ 2, 3 ]
```

With our `intersect()` function, we can still find the intersection between lists that have duplicate values. One downside to this approach is that it can't be done lazily because we're using `reduce()` to build a set. Another downside is that the code in our `reduce()` iteratee function isn't so straightforward.

Filtering list intersections

Let's implement another `intersect()` function that uses method chaining to filter out the intersecting list values:

```
const intersection = (...lists) =>
  List()
    .concat(...lists)
    .countBy(v => v)
    .toSeq()
    .filter(v => v === lists.length)
    .keySeq();
```

This is much easier to read. Let's break down what's happening here:

- `concat(...lists)`: This joins all list arguments together, resulting in one big list
- `countBy(v => v)`: This creates a map where the keys are the unique list values, and the map values are the number or occurrences in the list
- `toSeq()`: This enables lazy evaluation from this point forward
- `filter(v => v === lists.length)`: This finds intersecting values by checking if its count is the same as the number of lists passed to `intersect()`
- `keySeq()`: These are the actual values that intersect, since we've filtered out those that do not

Let's put this function to use now:

```
const myList1 = List.of(
  Map.of('first', 1, 'second', 2),
  Map.of('third', 3, 'fourth', 4)
);
const myList2 = List.of(
  Map.of('third', 3, 'fourth', 4),
  Map.of('fifth', 5, 'sixth', 6)
);
const myList3 = List.of(
```

```
    Map.of('first', 1, 'second', 2),
    Map.of('third', 3, 'fourth', 4),
    Map.of('seventh', 7, 'eighth', 8)
);

console.log('myList1', myList1.toJS());
// -> myList1 [ { first: 1, second: 2 }, { third: 3, fourth: 4 } ]
console.log('myList2', myList2.toJS());
// -> myList2 [ { third: 3, fourth: 4 }, { fifth: 5, sixth: 6 } ]
console.log('myList3', myList3.toJS());
// -> myList3 [ { first: 1, second: 2 },
// ->           { third: 3, fourth: 4 },
// ->           { seventh: 7, eighth: 8 } ]

intersection(myList1, myList2, myList3)
  .forEach((v) => {
    console.log('intersection', v.toJS());
  });
  // -> intersection { third: 3, fourth: 4 }
```

Now we have an `intersect()` function that is much easier to read because it follows the Immutable.js method chaining pattern using terse iteratee and predicate functions. It is also able to lazy filter the intersection values once the map with the counts is created.

The downside to this approach is that it does not work with duplicate values. You can make the trade off between our earlier implementation, which does allow duplicates, and this one, which does not. The reason this latter approach doesn't work with duplicate list values is because there would be no way to tell if the value exists in every list.

Collection differences

Differences are the inverse of intersections. They consist of all of the values that are not in every collection. If you add together the intersection and the difference, you get all of the collection values.

Set differences

Sets have a `subtract()` method, which can be used to find the difference between two sets. Here's an example:

```
const mySet1 = Set.of('first', 'second', 'third');
const mySet2 = Set.of('first', 'second');
const myDiff1 = mySet1.subtract(mySet2);
const myDiff2 = mySet2.subtract(mySet1);

console.log('mySet1', mySet1.toJS());
// -> mySet1 [ 'first', 'second', 'third' ]
console.log('mySet2', mySet2.toJS());
// -> mySet2 [ 'first', 'second' ]
console.log('myDiff1', myDiff1.toJS());
// -> myDiff1 [ 'third' ]
console.log('myDiff2', myDiff2.toJS());
// -> myDiff2 []
```

This method subtracts the set argument from the set on which the `subtract()` method is called. In `myDiff1`, you can see that the `'first'` and `'second'` values are the intersecting values between the two sets; so, when we use `subtract()`, we're essentially removing any intersecting values.

When we change the order around and call `subtract` on `mySet2`, using `mySet1` as the argument, there's no difference. This is because we're subtracting both the intersection and the difference from the result. This likely isn't the result that you want since there's clearly a difference between the two collections.

List differences

You can use the same technique that you used for finding list intersections to find list differences. Let's implement a `difference()` function:

```
const difference = (...lists) =>
  List()
    .concat(...lists)
    .countBy(v => v)
    .toSeq()
    .filter(v => v < lists.length)
    .keySeq();
```

This function will accept an arbitrary number of lists and find the values that aren't in every list. It uses the same approach as the `intersection()` function that we implemented earlier: count the values and filter out the values that have counts that are less than the number of lists passed. Here's the `difference()` function in use:

```
const myList1 = List.of(
  Map.of('first', 1, 'second', 2),
  Map.of('third', 3, 'fourth', 4)
);
const myList2 = List.of(
  Map.of('third', 3, 'fourth', 4),
  Map.of('fifth', 5, 'sixth', 6)
);
const myList3 = List.of(
  Map.of('first', 1, 'second', 2),
  Map.of('third', 3, 'fourth', 4),
  Map.of('seventh', 7, 'eighth', 8)
);

console.log('myList1', myList1.toJS());
// -> myList1 [ { first: 1, second: 2 }, { third: 3, fourth: 4 } ]
console.log('myList2', myList2.toJS());
// -> myList2 [ { third: 3, fourth: 4 }, { fifth: 5, sixth: 6 } ]
console.log('myList3', myList3.toJS());
// -> myList3 [ { first: 1, second: 2 },
// ->          { third: 3, fourth: 4 },
// ->          { seventh: 7, eighth: 8 } ]

difference(myList1, myList2, myList3)
  .forEach((v) => {
    console.log('first diff', v.toJS());
  });
  // -> first diff { first: 1, second: 2 }
  // -> first diff { fifth: 5, sixth: 6 }
  // -> first diff { seventh: 7, eighth: 8 }

difference(myList3, myList1, myList2)
  .forEach((v) => {
    console.log('second diff', v.toJS());
  });
  // -> second diff { first: 1, second: 2 }
  // -> second diff { seventh: 7, eighth: 8 }
  // -> second diff { fifth: 5, sixth: 6 }
```

Using this approach, we can use lists and lazily filter values that aren't in every list. It makes the assumption that values are unique within each list. It also doesn't matter in what order the list arguments are passed—the same difference is produced.

Comparing maps

When comparing lists or sets, you only have to worry about the collection values—indexes aren't in play. When comparing maps, you have to take both the key and its value into consideration.

Map intersections

Let's modify our intersection() function so that it works with maps. When we're looking for the intersection of two or more maps, the result should be another map with the intersecting key-value pairs. Here's the new version of intersection():

```
const intersection = (...maps) =>
  Map(List()
    .concat(...maps.map(m => m.entrySeq()))
    .map(List)
    .countBy(v => v)
    .toSeq()
    .filter(v => v === maps.length)
    .keySeq());
```

There are three differences between this implementation and the earlier implementation that works with lists:

- ...maps.map(m => m.entrySeq()): This turns every map into an array of key-value pair arrays.
- .map(List): This turns every key-value array into a key-value list so that countBy() will work correctly.
- Map(): Everything is wrapped in Map(), since this is what we want to return. The Map() constructor gets key-value pairs passed to it.

Now let's see this function in action:

```
const myMap1 = Map.of(
  'one', 1, 'two', 2, 'three', 3
);
const myMap2 = Map.of(
  'one', 1, 'three', 3, 'four', 4
);
const myMap3 = Map.of(
  'one', 1, 'two', 2, 'five', 5
);
```

```
console.log('intersection');
intersection(myMap1, myMap2, myMap3)
  .forEach((v, k) => console.log(k, v));
// -> intersection
// -> one 1
```

Map differences

The nicest part of the implementation strategy that we've been using with lists and maps so far in this chapter is that it's easy to change. With little effort, we were able to make the same `intersection()` function work with maps. To change the functionality from intersecting collections to finding the difference, we only needed to change the `filter()` predicate. Let's apply these changes to create a `difference()` function that works with maps:

```
const difference = (...maps) =>
  Map(List()
    .concat(...maps.map(m => m.entrySeq()))
    .map(List)
    .countBy(v => v)
    .filter(v => v < maps.length)
    .keySeq());
```

This looks just like the `intersection()` method that we just implemented for maps. The only change we've made here is to the `filter()` predicate. Let's see how this function works now:

```
console.log('difference');
difference(myMap1, myMap2, myMap3)
  .forEach((v, k) => console.log(k, v));
// -> difference
// -> two 2
// -> three 3
// -> four 4
// -> five 5
```

Most of the key-value pairs in `myMap1`, `myMap2`, and `myMap3` do not intersect, which is why they're returned from `difference()`.

Subsets and supersets

Immutable.js lists have a couple of complimentary methods that are handy for checking whether one list is part of another. Using these methods, you can avoid setting up your own elaborate reducing mechanism.

List subsets

If you want to know that a list belongs to another list, you can use the `isSubset()` method:

```
const myList = List.of(
  List.of(1, 2, 3),
  List.of(4, 5, 6),
  List.of(7, 8, 9)
);
const isSubset = List.of(1, 4, 7)
  .isSubset(myList.flatten());

console.log('isSubset', isSubset);
// -> isSubset true
```

The `myList` collection is a list of lists. So once you flatten it, you can pass it to the `isSubset()` method when it's called on the list: `List.of(1, 4, 7)`. This returns `true` because `myList` contains each of these values.

List supersets

The other approach is to use the `isSuperset()` method, which determines if the argument is a subset of the collection where we're calling the method:

```
const myList = List.of(
  List.of(1, 2, 3),
  List.of(4, 5, 6),
  List.of(7, 8, 9)
);
const isSuperset = myList
  .flatten()
  .isSuperset(List.of(2, 5, 8));

console.log('isSuperset', isSuperset);
// -> isSuperset true
```

As you can see, this is just another way of getting the same result as the prior example.

As a rule of thumb, if a collection is a subset of another collection, then the other collection is a superset. If a collection is a superset of another collection, then the other collection is a subset.

Summary

In this chapter, you learned about comparing collections. In Immutable.js applications, you can't always rely on simple equality with collections. Part of the collection might be equal to part of another collection, or you might want to compare more than two collections. The two main techniques that you learned were intersections and differences.

You implemented set intersections and differences using set methods. You then implemented the more involved intersection and difference functionality with lists. Then you implemented the intersection and difference functionality for maps.

In the following chapter, we'll look at ways that collections can be combined.

12
Combining Collections

There are times when you'll need to combine two or more Immutable.js collections into a single collection. This makes it much easier to design transformations, since they only have one collection on which to operate.

In this chapter, you'll learn the following approaches to combining collections:

- Merging maps
- Merging lists
- Concatenation
- Interposing
- Interleaving

Merging maps

Merging two or more maps together means that you want one map with key-value pairs from every map. The challenge comes where two of the maps have the same key.

Merging maps by key

When merging maps, there's always the chance that keys will conflict. The question is, which value gets used? Let's illustrate this idea by merging two simple lists together:

```
const myMap1 = Map.of(
  'one', 1, 'two', 2, 'three', 3
);
const myMap2 = Map.of(
  'two', 22, 'three', 33, 'four', 4
```

```
);
const myMergedMap = myMap1.merge(myMap2);

console.log('myMap1', myMap1.toJS());
// -> myMap1 { one: 1, two: 2, three: 3 }
console.log('myMap2', myMap2.toJS());
// -> myMap2 { two: 22, three: 33, four: 4 }
console.log('myMergedMap', myMergedMap.toJS());
// -> myMergedMap { one: 1, two: 22, three: 33, four: 4 }
```

As you can see, `myMergedMap` contains every key from `myMap1` and `myMap2`. There are two conflicting keys—`two` and `three`. By default, the `merge()` method will just override existing values. If you want to change this behavior, you have to use the `mergeWith()` method:

```
const myMergedWithMap = myMap1.mergeWith(
  v => v,
  myMap2
);

console.log('myMergedWithMap', myMergedWithMap.toJS());
// -> myMergedWithMap { one: 1, two: 2, three: 3, four: 4 }
```

The first argument that's passed to `mergeWith()` is a function that returns the value to use in case of a conflict. The function is passed to the two values of the conflicting key and the key itself as a third argument. In our case, we just want to use the old value when there's a conflict, so we just return the first argument.

> Other approaches to merging objects, such as `Object.assign()`, will actually mutate the first argument. To avoid this, you'll see empty objects passed as the first argument. Things like this aren't a concern in Immutable.js because any mutative method returns a new collection.

Merging maps with complex keys

Maps can have more complex values as keys, which means that you could have a trickier situation to deal with when there are merge conflicts. Let's reuse our previous example and change the keys into something more involved:

```
const myMap1 = Map.of(
  Map.of('name', 'one'), 1,
  Map.of('name', 'two'), 2,
  Map.of('name', 'three'), 3
);
```

```
const myMap2 = Map.of(
  Map.of('name', 'two'), 22,
  Map.of('name', 'three'), 33,
  Map.of('name', 'four'), 4
);
const myMergedMap = myMap1.merge(myMap2);
const myMergedWith = myMap1.mergeWith(
  v => v,
  myMap2
);

console.log('myMap1', myMap1.toJS());
// -> myMap1 { 'Map { "name": "one" }': 1,
// ->          'Map { "name": "two" }': 2,
// ->          'Map { "name": "three" }': 3 }
console.log('myMap2', myMap2.toJS());
// -> myMap2 { 'Map { "name": "two" }': 22,
// ->          'Map { "name": "three" }': 33,
// ->          'Map { "name": "four" }': 4 }
console.log('myMergedMap', myMergedMap.toJS());
// -> myMergedMap { 'Map { "name": "one" }': 1,
// ->               'Map { "name": "two" }': 22,
// ->               'Map { "name": "three" }': 33,
// ->               'Map { "name": "four" }': 4 }
console.log('myMergedWith', myMergedWith.toJS());
// -> myMergedWith { 'Map { "name": "one" }': 1,
// ->                'Map { "name": "two" }': 2,
// ->                'Map { "name": "three" }': 3,
// ->                'Map { "name": "four" }': 4 }
```

You use the exact same approach here—you use `mergeWith()` to deal with conflicts by just returning the original value. Key value conflicts are detected using deep equality, so it doesn't matter if you're merging maps with simple keys or with maps as keys.

Merging lists

Merging lists is a little different than merging maps. With maps, there's opportunity for conflict with keys that are equal. With lists, we're comparing index values when we merge. The likelihood for conflict when merging lists is high.

Merging simple values

Let's merge some simple list values using the `merge()` method:

```
const myList1 = List.of(1, 2, 3);
const myList2 = List.of(2, 3, 4, 5);
const myMergedList = myList1.merge(myList2);

console.log('myList1', myList1.toJS());
// -> myList1 [ 1, 2, 3 ]
console.log('myList2', myList2.toJS());
// -> myList2 [ 2, 3, 4, 5 ]
console.log('myMergedList', myMergedList.toJS());
// -> myMergedList [ 2, 3, 4, 5 ]
```

When we merge `myList1` and `myList2`, we have a conflict in index positions 0, 1, and 2. This is why the values 2, 3, and 4 are in `myMergedList`. The final value, 5, doesn't conflict with anything in `myList1`, so it will always end up in the merged result.

Once again, you might want to preserve the original values when there's a conflict. For this, you'll use the `mergeWith()` method again:

```
const myMergedWithList = myList1.mergeWith(
  (a, b) => a === undefined ? b : a,
  myList2
);

console.log('myMergedWithList', myMergedWithList.toJS());
// -> myMergedWithList [ 1, 2, 3, 5 ]
```

Unlike map merges, you actually need both of the `mergeWith()` iteratee arguments. You have to check to see if the first value, a, is undefined. This means that there's no index for the value in b, in which case we just want to return b. For example, the value 5 in `myList2` is at index 4. There's no index 4 value in `myList1`; so, this is how you add it to the merged result.

Let's try reversing the order of the two lists using our `mergeWith()` approach and see what happens:

```
const myMergedReversed = myList2.mergeWith(
  (a, b) => a === undefined ? b : a,
  myList1
);

console.log('myMergedReversed', myMergedReversed.toJS());
// -> myMergedReversed [ 2, 3, 4, 5 ]
```

This time, we're taking `myList2` and merging `myList1` into it. Every value in `myList1` has a conflict in `myList2`, so nothing from `myList1` is merged into `myMergedRevered`.

Merging lists of maps

Let's see what happens when we merge lists of maps:

```
const myList1 = List.of(
  Map.of('one', 1, 'two', 2),
  Map.of('three', 3, 'four', 4)
);
const myList2 = List.of(
  Map.of('one', 11, 'two', 22, 'three', 3),
  Map.of('four', 44, 'five', 5, 'size', 6)
);
const myMergedList = myList1.merge(myList2);

console.log('myList1', myList1.toJS());
// -> myList1 [ { one: 1, two: 2 }, { three: 3, four: 4 } ]
console.log('myList2', myList2.toJS());
// -> myList2 [ { one: 11, two: 22, three: 3 },
// ->           { four: 44, five: 5, size: 6 } ]
console.log('myMergedList', myMergedList.toJS());
// -> myMergedList [ { one: 11, two: 22, three: 3 },
// ->           { four: 44, five: 5, size: 6 } ]
```

The values from `myList2` override the values at the corresponding indexes in `myList1`. However, you don't want to preserve the values from `myList1` either. Instead, you'd prefer to merge the maps that are merged at the same index position:

```
const myMergedWithList = myList1.mergeWith(
  (a, b) => a.mergeWith(v => v, b),
  myList2
);

console.log('myMergedWithList', myMergedWithList.toJS());
// -> myMergedWithList [ { one: 1, two: 2, three: 3 },
// ->                    { three: 3, four: 4, five: 5, size: 6 } ]
```

This time around, we get the results we would expect. Using the `mergeWith()` iteratee function, we're able to call `mergeWith()` on the map in question.

Merging lists of lists

Merging lists of lists is a lot like merging lists of maps. The values from the second list override the values from the first list:

```
const myList1 = List.of(
  List.of(1, 2),
  List.of(3, 4)
);
const myList2 = List.of(
  List.of(11, 21, 3),
  List.of(33, 44, 5)
);
const myMergedList = myList1.merge(myList2);

console.log('myList1', myList1.toJS());
// -> myList1 [ [ 1, 2 ], [ 3, 4 ] ]
console.log('myList2', myList2.toJS());
// -> myList2 [ [ 11, 21, 3 ], [ 33, 44, 5 ] ]
console.log('myMergedList', myMergedList.toJS());
// -> myMergedList [ [ 11, 21, 3 ], [ 33, 44, 5 ] ]
```

Instead of replacing or preserving values, we want to merge the values that have the same index. Since these are lists instead of maps, the approach is slightly different:

```
const myMergedWithList = myList1.mergeWith(
  (a, b) => a.mergeWith((a1, b1) => a1 === undefined ? b1 : a1, b),
  myList2
);
console.log('myMergedWithList', myMergedWithList.toJS());
// -> myMergedWithList [ [ 1, 2, 3 ], [ 3, 4, 5 ] ]
```

Here, we get the expected result because we're properly merging lists inside of the `mergeWith()` iteratee.

Concatenating lists and sequences

If you have several lists that you need to run through a side-effect, it's usually a good choice to concatenate these lists together. It's easier for side-effects to iterate over one collection than several of them.

Simple value concatenation

The best way to think about concatenating lists together is as basic addition. You're effectively adding lists together, resulting in a larger list. You use the `concat()` method to concatenate lists:

```
const myList1 = List.of(1, 2, 3);
const myList2 = List.of(4, 5, 6);
const myList3 = List.of(7, 8, 9);
const myCombinedList = myList1.concat(
  myList2,
  myList3
);

console.log('myList1', myList1.toJS());
// -> myList1 [ 1, 2, 3 ]
console.log('myList2', myList2.toJS());
// -> myList2 [ 4, 5, 6 ]
console.log('myList3', myList3.toJS());
// -> myList3 [ 7, 8, 9 ]
console.log('myCombinedList', myCombinedList.toJS());
// -> myCombinedList [ 1, 2, 3, 4, 5, 6, 7, 8, 9 ]
```

Now our side-effect only needs to worry about iterating over `myCombinedList` instead of three individual lists.

Maps also have a `concat()` method that behaves identically to `merge()`. It's a good idea to stick with `merge()` for maps, to avoid confusion.

Lazy sequence concatenation

The challenge with the preceding approach is that the collections that we're concatenating together could actually be indexed sequences, capable of evaluating lazily. If you concatenate them into a list, then you lose any benefit to lazy evaluation. Instead, you can call the `concat()` method on a sequence:

```
const mySeq1 = Range(1, 6)
  .filterNot((v) => {
    console.log('mySeq1', v);
    return v % 2;
  });
const mySeq2 = Range(6, 11)
  .filterNot((v) => {
```

```
        console.log('mySeq2', v);
        return v % 2;
    });

Seq()
    .concat(mySeq1, mySeq2)
        .forEach(v => console.log('result', v));
        // -> mySeq1 1
        // -> mySeq1 2
        // -> result 2
        // -> mySeq1 3
        // -> mySeq1 4
        // -> result 4
        // -> mySeq1 5
        // -> mySeq2 6
        // -> result 6
        // -> mySeq2 7
        // -> mySeq2 8
        // -> result 8
        // -> mySeq2 9
        // -> mySeq2 10
        // -> result 10
```

Using this approach, you can lazily concatenate sequence values together as the `forEach()` side-effect iterates over the result. You can see how lazy evaluation works in the preceding example from the logging added in the `filterNot()` predicates.

Interposing and interleaving

Interposing means inserting the same value in-between every value in the indexed collection. **Interleaving** is like concatenation, except that the order of the resulting values is alternated between input lists based on the order of the collection arguments.

Lazily interposing values

Sometimes you need to separate your collection values using a static value. You could, for example, add this value to your side-effect as needed. The downside to this approach is that you would then have a side-effect code that now has to do something that's better handled by the Immutable.js chaining pattern.

Using the `interpose()` method, you can maintain the chainable method call pattern while passing separator data to your side-effects. Moreover, you can do this lazily as follows:

```
const myList = List.of(1, 2, 3, 4, 5, 6, 7, 8);

myList
  .toSeq()
  .filter((v) => {
    console.log('filtering', v);
    return v % 2;
  })
  .interpose('...')
  .forEach(v => console.log(v));
// -> filtering 1
// -> 1
// -> filtering 2
// -> filtering 3
// -> ...
// -> 3
// -> filtering 4
// -> filtering 5
// -> ...
// -> 5
// -> filtering 6
// -> filtering 7
// -> ...
// -> 7
// -> filtering 8
```

Now, your `forEach()` side-effect that renders this list has the . . . strings interposed in between every value. The `filter()` logging is added so that you can see how these values are lazily added to your sequence. When you decide that you no longer need this functionality, all you have to do is to delete one line from your method call chain. No changes to the side-effect code are necessary.

Lazily interleaving values

Interleaving sequence values is useful when you're looking for a value in more than one sequence. This makes it easy to look in every collection without having to search one collection entirely before moving on to the next one:

```
const myList1 = List.of(1, 2, 3);
const myList2 = List.of(4, 5, 6);
const myList3 = List.of(7, 8, 9);
```

```
console.log('found', myList1
  .toSeq()
  .interleave(myList2, myList3)
  .find((v) => {
    console.log('checking', v);
    return v === 7;
}));
// -> checking 1
// -> checking 4
// -> checking 7
// -> found 7
```

As the logging shows, you only have to check the values 1 and 4 before finding the value you're looking for. Because you have interleaved the lists using `interleave()`, you avoid having to check 2, 3, 5, and 6.

Summary

In this chapter, you learned how to combine Immutable.js collections, starting with merging maps together. When maps are merged, there are usually conflicts with keys. You get to decide what happens when there's a conflict. When merging lists, conflicts are based on indexes and these need to be dealt with accordingly.

We then looked at concatenating lists of values. Side-effects have an easier time dealing with one collection instead of several collections. You can lazily concatenate collections using sequences so that you don't have to allocate new collections.

Interposing values into collections means putting the same value in-between every collection value. Interleaving collections balances the placement of values from several collections into one collection.

In the next chapter, you'll see how we can use immutable collections to help us write better declarative code.

13
Declarative Decision Making

Thinking of Immutable.js as a tool for dealing strictly with IO data in your applications is easy. Indeed, this is a key role for the library. However, you can also leverage immutable collections to assist you with using a declarative programming style that leads to more maintainable code. In this chapter, you'll do the following:

- Using maps as the core mechanism to decide which behavior to execute
- Parameterizing behaviors and providing default behaviors
- Composing complex behaviors out of simple behaviors

Mapping behavior

In imperative code, you have things, such as `if` statements, that determine what happens next. Taken in moderation, there's nothing wrong with this type of construct. But when your main avenue of logic is imperative statements, things tend to grow unmaintainable quickly.

The alternative to this imperative style is to compose your logic declaratively. Maps are the first tool that will help you get there.

Keys are logical paths, values are behavior

When you use maps as the means to declare your application logic, it's helpful to think of the map keys as the possible paths. For example, an `if` statement checks whether a condition is true, and if so, it allows for a block of code to be executed. With maps, keys are the condition. The values with which they're paired represent the functionality to execute when the condition is true.

Let's illustrate this idea at it's most basic level using an Immutable.js map:

```
const actions = Map.of(
  'first', () => console.log('first'),
  'second', () => console.log('second'),
  'third', () => console.log('third')
);

actions.get('second')();
// -> second
actions.get('third')();
// -> third
```

The `actions` map represents the possible actions taken. The keys are the logical paths through your program and the values are the functions that run at the appropriate time. In this example, the correct string is logged based on what is passed to `actions.get()`. Here's another way to write this code:

```
if (action === 'first') {
  console.log('first');
} else if (action === 'second') {
  console.log('second');
} else if (action === 'third') {
  console.log('third');
}
```

This code works fine. It's just that it becomes difficult to manage as more and more cases need to be added. It's hard to break branching statements down into little portable units that can be called in different contexts the same way that you can with mapped behaviors.

Wrapping behavior maps in functions

Calling `get()` directly on a map in order to run the appropriate behaviors is unlikely. Instead, you can wrap the `Map` declaration and the `get()` function together into a function. Then you can call the function with the key that determines which behavior will run, as shown here:

```
const myBehavior = action => Map.of(
  'first', () => console.log('first'),
  'second', () => console.log('second'),
  'third', () => console.log('third')
).get(action)();
```

Now you can pass an action to `myBehavior()`, and the corresponding path is followed through the map:

```
myBehavior('first');
// -> first
myBehavior('second');
// -> second
```

By calling `myBehavior()`, you're also calling the corresponding function from the map that's looked up by the key. But what happens when there is no path and, therefore, no behavior? Let's find out:

```
myBehavior();
// -> TypeError: Map.of(...).get(...) is not a function
```

This happens because we're passing `get()` a nonexistent key. This results in an `undefined` value being returned. An exception is thrown because we're trying to call `undefined` as if it were a function.

Parameters and defaults

The preceding example has a couple of limitations. First, there's no way to pass arguments to the behaviors when they're called. Second, if you try to call something that doesn't exist, it blows up. We should be able to address both of these issues.

Providing default behavior

When the caller attempts to call a behavior that doesn't exist by passing a key that doesn't exist in the behavior map, you should be able to recover from this. Thankfully, the `get()` method accepts a second argument that's returned if the requested key doesn't exist:

```
const myBehavior = action => Map.of(
  true, () => console.log('thruth'),
  false, () => console.log('lies')
).get(
  action,
  () => console.log('default')
)();

myBehavior(true);
// -> truth
myBehavior(false);
// -> lies
```

```
myBehavior();
// -> default
myBehavior(123);
// -> default
```

The last two calls to `myBehavior()` result in the default behavior running because neither call is passed a key that exists. This means that the second value passed to `get()` is returned, which in this case is a function that logs `'default'`. In practice, this function could be a no-op, or something specific to the application you're building.

Parameterizing mapped behavior

If you could pass arguments to the behavior that gets invoked when you call your behavior functions, it would be nice. This would mean that your behavior function would have to forward the arguments that it receives to the functions that it looks up from the behavior map:

```
const log = value => console.log('log:', value);
const myBehavior = (action, ...args) => Map.of(
  'start', value => log(`starting ${value}...`),
  'stop', value => log(`stopping ${value}...`)
).get(
  action,
  () => {}
)(...args);

myBehavior('start', 'database');
// -> log: starting database...
myBehavior('start', 'server');
// -> log: starting server...
myBehavior('stop', 'database');
// -> log: stopping database...
myBehavior('stop', 'server');
// -> log: stopping server...
```

Here, we updated the signature of `myBehavior()` to include an `args` rest parameter. It's called a **rest parameter** because the `...` syntax allows `args` to capture an arbitrary number of arguments if they're passed. Then, we use the **spread operator** (`...`) to forward these arguments to the behavior functions once they've been looked up.

In this example, the first argument is used to look up the behavior to execute, and the second string parameter is passed to the behavior function which is then logged.

Composing behavior

So far, we've been able to encapsulate mapped behaviors inside of a function. But in order to build complex applications, you need a means to compose larger behavior out of smaller behavior.

A generic higher-order behavior function

You can enhance the approach we've been following so far with our mapped behavior to produce a higher-order function: a function that returns other functions. For example, we've been creating new `Map` instances every time we invoke behavior, which is unnecessary. If we return a new function, we don't have to store our mapped behavior anywhere—we just have to pass it in as an argument:

```
const behavior = (behaviors, defaultBehavior = () => {}) =>
  (action, ...args) =>
    behaviors.get(action, defaultBehavior)(...args);
```

The `behavior()` higher-order function returns a new function that can be called with a given `action` and arguments to forward to the behavior. The `behaviors` argument is a map used to look up behavior based on the `action` argument. The `defaultBehavior` argument is called if the action isn't found in the map. This is a no-op function by default, but you can pass in your own default behavior. Let's build a couple of functions using `behavior()`:

```
const greaterThanFive = behavior(Map.of(
  true, n => `${n} is greater than 5`,
  false, n => `${n} is less than 5`
));
const lessThanTen = behavior(Map.of(
  true, n => `${n} is less than 10`,
  false, n => `${n} is greater than 10`
));
```

Here we have two functions that take actions based on a Boolean value. For example, the `greaterThanFive()` function accepts a Boolean value and a number as arguments, and it will log different strings based on these values. Let's see these two functions in action now:

```
const a = 6;
const b = 1;
const c = 12;

console.log(greaterThanFive(a > 5, a));
// -> 6 is greater than 5
```

```
console.log(lessThanTen(a < 10, a));
// -> 6 is less than 10
console.log(greaterThanFive(b > 5, b));
// -> 1 is less than 5
console.log(lessThanTen(c < 10, c));
// -> 12 is greater than 10
```

We get the expected results here, depending on the Boolean value that's passed. We still have a couple of things to improve with this approach, though. For one thing, the Boolean expressions are passed directly to the function, which might be awkward to write after a while. Another issue is that we need a way to stitch these behavioral functions together.

Logical and/or conditions

You've seen how we can use maps to execute behavior based on a single value. Where this approach falls apart is when you get into more involved logic and/or conditions. However, you can still use Immutable.js collections to check declaratively for these types of conditions. For example, let's implement a function that will help us look for AND/OR conditions:

```
const some = (...predicates) => {
  const predicateSeq = Seq(predicates);
  return (...args) => predicateSeq.some(p => p(...args));
};
const every = (...predicates) => {
  const predicateSeq = Seq(predicates);
  return (...args) => predicateSeq.every(p => p(...args));
};
```

The some() function is used to evaluate predicate functions in a logical OR fashion while the every() function evaluates predicate functions in a logical AND fashion. Both functions follow the same approach—they just use different sequence methods to return the result.

The idea is to construct a sequence (predicateSeq) from the predicate function arguments (predicates). Then we use the some()/every() method to call each predicate function with the given behavior arguments. The some() method returns true the first time that a predicate function returns true. The every() method returns true only if every predicate returns true. Let's use these functions to compose some behavior:

```
const hasEnough = some(
  v => v.get('source1') > 5,
  v => v.get('source2') > 5,
  v => v.get('source3') > 5
```

```
);
const hasEverything = every(
  v => v.get('enabled'),
  v => v.get('hasPermission'),
  v => v.get('oldEnough')
);
```

Now we have two functions that we can call to test logical AND/OR conditions. In the
hasEnough() function, we have three predicates that test the values of different map
properties. If any of these return true, hasEnough() will return true. The
hasEverything() function also has three predicates, but will only return true if every
predicate returns true.

Now let's compose some behavior to execute side-effects based on the result of calling
hasEnough() and hasEverything():

```
const logHasEnough = behavior(Map.of(
  true, () => console.log('yep, has enough'),
  false, () => console.log('sorry, not enough')
));
const logHasEverything = behavior(Map.of(
  true, () => console.log('yep, has everything'),
  false, () => console.log('sorry, not everything')
));
```

Once again, we have functions that map Boolean input values to behavior. In this case,
we're executing logging side-effects. Let's test out what we have:

```
const myMap1 = Map.of(
  'source1', 5,
  'source2', 6,
  'source3', 7
);
const myMap2 = Map.of(
  'source1', 6
);
const myMap3 = Map.of(
  'source1', 1,
  'source2', 2,
  'source3', 3
);
const myMap4 = Map.of(
  'enabled', true,
  'hasPermission', true,
  'oldEnough', true
);
const myMap5 = Map.of(
```

```
  'enabled', true,
  'hasPermission', true
);

console.log('myMap1', myMap1.toJS());
logHasEnough(hasEnough(myMap1));
// -> myMap1 { source1: 5, source2: 6, source3: 7 }
// -> yep, has enough
console.log('myMap2', myMap2.toJS());
logHasEnough(hasEnough(myMap2));
// -> myMap2 { source1: 6 }
// -> yep, has enough
console.log('myMap3', myMap3.toJS());
logHasEnough(hasEnough(myMap3));
// -> myMap3 { source1: 1, source2: 2, source3: 3 }
// -> sorry, not enough
console.log('myMap4', myMap4.toJS());
logHasEverything(hasEverything(myMap4));
// -> myMap4 { enabled: true, hasPermission: true, oldEnough: true }
// -> yep, has everything
console.log('myMap5', myMap5.toJS());
logHasEverything(hasEverything(myMap5));
// -> myMap5 { enabled: true, hasPermission: true }
// -> sorry, not everything
```

We've managed to distill our logic, and the code that runs as a result, into two function calls. We have a function that evaluates to Boolean result, and a function executes based on this result. As your application grows and more conditions become necessary, it's easier to expand this declarative code than it would be to hunt down if statements.

Complex behavior compositions

The final piece of this logic puzzle involves gluing these AND/OR conditions together. Luckily, we've already built all of the infrastructure to do this. For example, if you want to compose a new function that checks for both hasEnough() and hasEverything(), you can do so as follows:

```
const hasBoth = every(
  hasEnough,
  hasEverything
);
```

The `hasBoth()` function that we've just created will only return `true` if both `hasEnough()` and `hasEverything()` return `true`. Let's put this new function to work and tie this all together:

```
const logHasBoth = behavior(Map.of(
  true, () => console.log('yep, it has all of it'),
  false, () => console.log('nope')
));
const myMap6 = myMap1.merge(myMap4);
const myMap7 = myMap1.merge(myMap5);

console.log('myMap6', myMap6.toJS());
logHasBoth(hasBoth(myMap6));
// -> myMap6 { source1: 5, source2: 6,
// ->          source3: 7, enabled: true,
// ->          hasPermission: true, oldEnough: true }
// -> yep, it has all of it
console.log('myMap7', myMap7.toJS());
logHasBoth(hasBoth(myMap7));
// -> myMap6 { source1: 5, source2: 6,
// ->          source3: 7, enabled: true,
// ->          hasPermission: true }
// -> nope
```

With the tools that we've created in this chapter, you have everything you need to compose new behavior in a declarative way that's easy to understand and maintain.

Summary

In this chapter, you learned how to use Immutable.js collections as a tool to aid in declarative decision making. Maps are the foundation of this idea, because you can use them to look up a behavior to run based on keys. They also allow you to run default behavior when nothing is found—kind of like an `else` block.

You also learned how to compose complex behavior that models logical AND/OR decisions. Once again, Immutable.js collection methods helped us here. With these two things in place, you composed complex application behavior in an easy-to-understand way.

In the next chapter, we'll use side-effects to render actual UI elements.

14
Side-Effects in User Interfaces

Without side-effects, Immutable.js code wouldn't be able to interact with the outside world. Collections by themselves can only produce new data—they can't display data on the screen. To do this type of thing, you need side-effects. In this chapter, we'll cover two different approaches to rendering user interfaces using Immutable.js side-effects:

- Rendering using native DOM APIs
- Rendering using React

A simple application

To demonstrate how Immutable.js applications use side-effects to render UI components, we'll build a very simple application that lists Black Mirror episodes and provides a handful of filter controls. We'll build the exact same user interface using DOM APIs and then do so again with React.

Application data

The application data that we will be rendering is a list of Black Mirror episodes. Each episode is a map with some information about the episode. Here's a truncated version of the list to give you an idea of what it looks like as an Immutable.js collection:

```
const episodes = List.of(
  Map.of(
    'title', 'The National Anthem',
    'date', 'December 4 2011',
    'director', 'Otto Bathurst',
    'rating', 8.0
  ),
```

```
    Map.of(
      'title', 'Fifteen Million Merits',
      'date', 'December 11 2011',
      'director', 'Euros Lyn',
      'rating', 8.3
    ),
    Map.of(
      'title', 'The Entire History of You',
      'date', 'December 18 2011',
      'director', 'Brian Welsh',
      'rating', 8.7
    ),
    Map.of(
      'title', 'Be Right Back',
      'date', 'February 1 2013',
      'director', 'Owen Harris',
      'rating', 8.2
    ),
    ...
  );
```

By default, your application will display everything in this list. Your job is to implement filter controls that filter this list before it is rendered, based on how the user interacts with the filter controls.

Filter controls

To help your users filter the list of episodes that are rendered, you'll provide a search text input box that will allow them to search episodes. As they type, the displayed episodes are updated to reflect the search string. You'll also provide checkboxes that allow the user to specify which fields of an episode are searched. Finally, you'll provide a range slider that allows the user to specify the minimum rating of an episode to be included in results. Here's what the filter controls look like:

Episode results

Listed below the filter controls are the actual episodes. This is a simple list, where each item displays details about the episode:

The idea of this simple application is to use the same Immutable.js collection data and filtering techniques in different styles of UI implementations. The side-effects required to render this collection data are different from those needed to render it using React components. However, your Immutable.js code should be recognizable no matter how it's used by side-effects.

DOM side-effects

In this version of our user interface, the side-effects will interact directly with DOM APIs. First, we'll create the overall HTML structure of the UI. Then we'll implement the application logic.

HTML markup

There are three areas that make up this user interface: the `filter` fields, the rating slider, and the episode listing. Each of these areas will have initial HTML rendered before any JavaScript runs.

Filter fields

To search through episodes, the user is presented with a text input:

```
<input placeholder="filter" type="search" autofocus/>
```

Below the `search` text input are fields that they can select. These fields represent where the `search` control is looking:

```
<ul>
  <li>
    <label>
      Title
      <input type="checkbox" name="title" checked/>
    </label>
  </li>
  <li>
    <label>
      Date
      <input type="checkbox" name="date"/>
    </label>
  </li>
  <li>
```

```
    <label>
      Director
      <input type="checkbox" name="director"/>
    </label>
  </li>
</ul>
```

Each of these checkboxes represents a key in the episode maps. If the checkbox is checked, you have to include this particular key in your filtering operation. By default, only the Title filter field is selected.

Rating slider

To filter episodes by rating, we provide the user with a slider that's used to indicate the minimum rating:

```
<label>
  7
  <input type="range" min="1" max="10" value="7" name="rating"/>
</label>
```

Episodes with a rating lower than this value are excluded from the results. By default, the minimum rating is set to 7. The label is used to indicate the current slider value.

Episode template

Our side-effect will need to insert new HTML elements. For every episode that makes it through the filter, we'll have to insert it into the DOM. For this, we'll use a template element, since we'll have to insert many copies of this HTML fragment:

```
<template id="episode-template">
  <li>
    <header>
      <h4></h4>
    </header>
    <section>
      <p><strong>Date: </strong> </p>
      <p><strong>Director: </strong> </p>
      <p><strong>Rating: </strong> </p>
    </section>
  </li>
</template>
```

There are a couple of important details about the structure of this HTML to note here. First, the <h4> tag is empty. Second, each <p> tag has a space at the end of it. In both cases, we'll fill in these blanks with text when we run our side-effects.

Filtering episodes

Let's address the most important part of our application first—filtering episodes. We have search text input and a rating to consider. We also have the filter fields to consider, which change the way the search text is used. To compose our filter behavior, we'll borrow some ideas from Chapter 13, *Declarative Decision Making*:

```
const some = (...predicates) => {
  const predicateSeq = Seq(predicates);
  return (...args) => predicateSeq.some(p => p(...args));
};
const every = (...predicates) => {
  const predicateSeq = Seq(predicates);
  return (...args) => predicateSeq.every(p => p(...args));
};
```

Both of these functions are higher-order functions—they take functions as arguments and use them to compose and return a new function. The some() function is used to implement OR logic while the every() function is used to implement AND logic. Inside of these functions, we're creating sequences and calling their respective some() and every() methods to get the result we need.

With these two functions in place, we're almost ready to compose a filtering function. We just need the DOM nodes that have the values of the filter fields, because we need to know which map values to check and what the minimum rating should be:

```
const title = document.querySelector('input[name="title"]');
const date = document.querySelector('input[name="date"]');
const director = document.querySelector('input[name="director"]');
const rating = document.querySelector('input[name="rating"]');
```

Now we can compose our `filter()` function:

```
const filter = query => every(
  some(
    () => query === undefined,
    () => query === '',
    every(
      () => title.checked,
      v => v.get('title').includes(query)
    ),
    every(
      () => date.checked,
      v => v.get('date').includes(query)
    ),
    every(
      () => director.checked,
      v => v.get('director').includes(query)
    )
  ),
  v => v.get('rating') >= (+rating.value)
);
```

The `filter()` function that we've just implemented accepts a `query` argument and returns a new function that we can use to filter collections. As you can see, we have three levels of `every()`/`some()` calls, so let's walk through what they're doing.

The outermost call to `every()` is making sure that both the query string and the rating return `true` for a given map. The call to `some()` is checking the query string against the map values of a given episode. So if any of these fields match, we return `true`, including an empty or undefined `query` argument. The deepest calls to `every()` are how we check if a given map key should be searched. For example, if `director.checked` is `false`, it means that the user hasn't selected the `director` checkbox and this field should not be searched.

Handling events

In order to invoke our filtering behavior in response to user interactions, we have to write some code that responds to user input. This includes the following:

- Responding to input events when the user types in the search box
- Responding to change events when the user checks/unchecks field checkboxes
- Responding to rating slider change events

Before we write our handler functions for these events, let's think about how we want to compose them. We want to avoid imperative-style `if` statements, as this can make our code fragile and difficult to change. The common case is to check for several conditions and, if they're all `true`, execute behavior for the handler. We already have the `some()` and `every()` functions ready to go. But these alone don't quite get us what we need. Let's bring in our `behavior()` function from Chapter 13, *Declarative Decision Making*, and use it with `every()` to create another higher-order tool for our event handlers:

```
const behavior = (behaviors, defaultBehavior = () => {}) =>
  (action, ...args) =>
    behaviors.get(action, defaultBehavior)(...args);
const everyThen = (func, ...predicates) =>
  (...args) => behavior(Map.of(
    true, func
  ))(every(...predicates)(...args), ...args);
```

Here, we're creating a slightly different version of the `every()` function, with the help of `behavior()`. The idea with `everyThen()` is to return a function that calls `func()` only when every predicate is `true`. It can be thought of as "if *every* predicate is `true`, *then* call this function." Let's use this tool to compose our event handlers, as follows:

```
const search = document.querySelector('input[type="search"]');

document.addEventListener('input', everyThen(
  e => render(e.target.value),
  e => e.target instanceof HTMLInputElement,
  e => e.target.type === 'search'
));
document.addEventListener('change', everyThen(
  () => render(search.value),
  e => e.target instanceof HTMLInputElement,
  e => [
    'title',
    'date',
    'director',
    'rating'
  ].includes(e.target.name)
));
document.addEventListener('change', everyThen(
  (e) => {
    e.target.parentNode.childNodes[0].nodeValue = e.target.value;
  },
  e => e.target instanceof HTMLInputElement,
  e => e.target.name === 'rating'
));
```

As you can see, we've set up three event handlers using `everyThen()`. The first argument is the function that's actually called in response to the event, provided that the other arguments return `true`. Here's a breakdown of the event handlers we just created:

- Responding to the user typing in the search box and rendering the episode results
- Responding to any of the filter checkboxes or the rating slider and rendering the episode results
- Responding to the rating slider and updating the text of the adjacent label with the slider value

Rendering elements

At this point, we've set up everything we need except for the actual side-effect that renders episodes. We've encapsulated this into a function since it's called in several places:

```
const render = (query) => {
  while (results.firstChild) {
    results.removeChild(results.firstChild);
  }
  episodes
    .filter(filter(query))
    .forEach((v) => {
      const { content } = episodeTemplate;
      const episodeTitle = content.querySelector('h4');
      const episodeDate = content.querySelector('p:nth-of-type(1)');
      const episodeDirector = content.querySelector('p:nth-of-type(2)');
      const episodeRating = content.querySelector('p:nth-of-type(3)');

      episodeTitle.textContent = v.get('title');
      episodeDate.childNodes[1].nodeValue = v.get('date');
      episodeDirector.childNodes[1].nodeValue = v.get('director');
      episodeRating.childNodes[1].nodeValue = v.get('rating');
      results.appendChild(document.importNode(content, true));
    });
};
```

We're calling our `filter()` function, giving it a query string, and passing the resulting function to the `filter()` method. Then, the `forEach()` iteratee carries out the side-effect. First, we empty out any existing episodes that were rendered previously. Then we use `episodeTemplate` to create new DOM nodes and insert them into the document, based on results returned from the filter operation.

React side-effects

Now we'll implement the exact same UI using React. The aim is to illustrate that Immutable.js collections are helpful as the only library, or as a utility alongside many other libraries.

Application state

Application state in the previous example was kept in the DOM itself. For example, we had to query the DOM for checkbox nodes if we wanted to see if one of them was selected. With React components, state belongs in a component. Since our application is a simple one, we only need a single container, the app itself:

```
class App extends React.Component {
  constructor() {
    super();
    this.state = {
      episodes,
      query: '',
      title: true,
      date: false,
      director: false,
      rating: 7
    };
  }
  ...
}
```

React component state is stored in a `state` property of the component when it is created. The `episodes` value that you see here is the same episode list from the previous example. Now, it's part of this `App` component's state. The other values here represent the state of HTML elements. For example, the Boolean values represent the state of the checkboxes.

Handling events and changing state

When our UI is first loaded, we'll need to bootstrap this `App` component. This is done using the `ReactDOM.render()` method:

```
ReactDOM.render(<App />, document.getElementById('app')};
```

This JSX syntax is unique to React. This renders the `App` component into the `#app` element. This causes the `render()` method to be called. This will return the same markup that's used in the preceding example. Here's the JSX for the search input element:

```
<input
  placeholder="filter"
  type="search"
  value={this.state.query}
  autoFocus
  onInput={e => this.setState({
    query: e.target.value
  })}
/>
```

The value of this input is set to the `query` state of this component. The `onInput` event handler changes the state of the component. Specifically, it sets the `query` state, which causes the `render()` method to be called. The nice thing about this style of event handlers is that they're highly focused, setting the state of the component and letting the React machinery do the rest. Here's one of the checkbox elements:

```
<label>
  Title
  <input
    type="checkbox"
    checked={this.state.title}
    onChange={e => this.setState({
      title: e.target.checked
    })}
  />
</label>
```

The same approach is used here. The state of the DOM node is managed by the state of the React component. The state of the React component is manipulated by the event handlers.

Mapping episodes to elements

The actual side-effect that renders the episode results is similar, but with a few React subtleties. For one thing, the `filter()` function that composes the `filter()` iteratee is now a method of the app component:

```
class App extends React.Component {
  filter(query) {
    return every(
      some(
        () => query === undefined,
```

```
          () => query === '',
          every(
            () => this.state.title,
            v => v.get('title').includes(query)
          ),
          every(
            () => this.state.date,
            v => v.get('date').includes(query)
          ),
          every(
            () => this.state.director,
            v => v.get('director').includes(query)
          )
        ),
        v => v.get('rating') >= (+this.state.rating)
      );
    }
    ...
}
```

This is necessary because instead of depending on DOM nodes for state, we need to check things such as `this.state.director`.

Another difference is that instead of using an HTML `<template>` element to help render episodes, we've implemented an `Episode` component:

```
const Episode = props => (
  <li>
    <header>
      <h4>{props.title}</h4>
    </header>
    <section>
      <p><strong>Date: </strong>{props.date}</p>
      <p><strong>Director: </strong>{props.director}</p>
      <p><strong>Rating: </strong>{props.rating}</p>
    </section>
  </li>
);
```

Instead of state, this component relies on property values passed to it from its parent component. Here's the side-effect from our episode collection that uses the `Episode` component:

```
<ul id="results">
  {this.state.episodes
    .filter(this.filter(this.state.query))
    .toJS()
    .map(v => (<Episode key={v.title} {...v} />))}
</ul>
```

The `filter()` method is called the exact same way as as it was in the previous example. But now we're calling `toJS()`, which converts our list of maps into an array of objects. The reason that we have to do this is because we need an array of `<Episode>` components, not a list of them. Calling `map()` on an array ensures that we pass an array of components to `{ }`, like JSX expects.

Summary

This chapter introduced you to the concept of using side-effects from Immutable.js method call chains to render UI elements. We first looked at how to do this using nothing but Immutable.js and native DOM methods. Using the techniques for composing behavior that you learned in `Chapter 13`, *Declarative Decision Making*, you composed event handling behavior and filtering behavior for the episodes to render.

You then implemented the same UI using the same Immutable.js techniques, but now using React as the UI component library. In the end, it doesn't matter what tooling you're using in your application—the tools and techniques you've learned about Immutable.js are universally applicable.

In the next chapter, we'll continue our discussion on side-effects, except we'll shift the focus to Node.js environments.

15
Side-Effects in Node.js

In Node.js environments, the majority of side-effects come in the form of IO. This is what Node.js excels at—orchestrating huge volumes of IO operations. This is why it has a stream API that most IO components implement.

In this chapter, we'll look at Immutable.js collections from the perspective of Node.js IO. You'll learn how to do the following:

- Reading and parsing CSV data into Immutable.js collections
- Handling the parsing of lots of input data
- Iterating over collections to write data
- Writing collection values asynchronously to streams
- Chaining streams together and lazily processing Immutable.js sequences

Reading data into collections

The first step toward making use of Immutable.js collections in Node.js applications is reading data into them. You can read and parse CSV data into lists of maps, for example. When you start to read large amounts of data, things become trickier because things happen asynchronously.

Reading and parsing CSV data

Let's say that you have the following CSV data that you want to parse and use in an Immutable.js collection:

```
one,1,two,2,three,3
four,4,five,5,six,6
seven,7,eight,8,nine,9
```

Each row is a map that you want to insert into a list. Luckily, the format of each of these rows is already something that you can pass to `Map.of()`. You just need to parse it. To help with this, we'll use the `readline` module. This works by passing it a readable stream, and in return, it emits the `line` events every time a line is parsed. From there, you just have to create the map and add it to your list, as follows:

```
let myMapList = List();

const csvInput = readline.createInterface({
  input: fs.createReadStream('./input/01-data.csv')
});

csvInput.on('line', (line) => {
  myMapList = myMapList.push(
    Map.of(...line.split(','))
  );
});

csvInput.on('close', () => {
  console.log('myMapList', myMapList.toJS());
});
// -> myMapList [ { one: '1', two: '2', three: '3' },
// ->            { four: '4', five: '5', six: '6' },
// ->            { seven: '7', eight: '8', nine: '9' } ]
```

With each line that's parsed and emitted with the `line` event, we assign a new list to `myMapList` by calling the `push()` method to add a new map. The coolest part of this example is that you can use the spread operator to prepare the arguments that get passed to `Map.of()`—you don't have to do anything else with the line once it's read.

Reading large amounts of data

The previous example emitted events for every line read. This approach doesn't scale as well when you're dealing with larger volumes of input data. For example, what if many lines were read? Shouldn't you process these at the same time? The first step is listening to the `data` event on the readable stream instead of using the `readline` module.

The file we'll use as input for these examples will be the standard `words` file that's found in one place or another on Unix systems. This gives us ~235,000 lines to work with.

Using concat()

The challenge with the `data` event is that the chunk of data that it gives to our event handler isn't something that's parsable. For example, it could leave off half of a word. This is no big deal—we'll just have to account for this:

```
let myWordList = List();
let last = '';

console.time('elapsed');
const wordInput = fs.createReadStream('./input/words');

wordInput.on('data', (data) => {
  const words = (last + data.toString()).split(os.EOL);
  last = words[words.length - 1];

  myWordList = myWordList.concat(words.slice(0, words.length - 1));
});

wordInput.on('end', () => {
  console.log('word count', myWordList.count().toLocaleString());
  console.timeEnd('elapsed');
  // -> word count 235,886
  // -> elapsed: 2012.116ms
});
```

The data that's passed to the handler function as an argument is just a small chunk of the overall stream. So, since we don't know where this chunk cuts off, we have to assume that the last word has missing characters. We store the last word so that we can join it with the next chunk. Then we concatenate the words with `myWordList`. Based on the timer we've set up, this takes about 2 seconds to complete. Can we do better than this?

Using push()

The `data` event allows us to process data as it becomes available. However, concatenating the values to our list can be a real bottleneck—especially when we're working with thousands of items. Let's change our approach from using `concat()` to using `push()` to build the list, as follows:

```
wordInput.on('data', (data) => {
  const words = `${last}${data.toString()}`.split(os.EOL);
  last = words[words.length - 1];

  for (const word of words) {
    myWordList = myWordList.push(word);
  }
});

wordInput.on('end', () => {
  console.log('word count', myWordList.count().toLocaleString());
  console.timeEnd('elapsed');
  // -> word count 235,886
  // -> elapsed: 959.299ms
});
```

You would think that `concat()` has an advantage over `push()` because it can add many values to collections without having to create several intermediary collection instances. In this example, every time we call `push()`, we're creating a new collection, which can get expensive. With `concat()`, we're only creating one new collection, but the work performed inside of `concat()` is clearly more expensive than creating new collections with `push()`. Can we do better still?

Using push() and withMutations()

On its own, the `push()` method is inexpensive in terms of CPU time or memory allocations. Where it gets expensive is when calling it over and over in a loop, as we've done in the previous example. Let's fix this so that we can use the `push()` method approach without having to keep allocating new collections:

```
wordInput.on('data', (data) => {
  const words = `${last}${data.toString()}`.split(os.EOL);
  last = words[words.length - 1];

  myWordList = myWordList.withMutations((list) => {
    for (const word of words) {
      list.push(word);
```

```
    }
  });
});

wordInput.on('end', () => {
  console.log('word count', myWordList.count().toLocaleString());
  console.timeEnd('elapsed');
  // -> word count 235,886
  // -> elapsed: 806.099ms
});
```

Using the `withMutations()` method, we've managed to shave more time off our `push()` approach. This method allows us to use mutative collection methods, without having to assign new collections. As you can see, we're just calling `push()` without assigning the return value to anything.

> Don't overuse `withMutations()`. Save it for the performance-sensitive areas of your code, where creating intermediary collections slows things down. Using it everywhere accomplishes nothing other than diluting the value of your functional code. Also be sure to check with the Immutable.js documentation to make sure that the method can safely be used inside `withMutations()`, because not every method can.

Writing collection data

To write data from Immutable.js collections to an output stream, we set up a side-effect that iterates over the collection, writing each value to the stream. In simple cases, this is easy to do. In the more complex cases, you have to pay attention to concurrent and lazy evaluation.

Iterating over collections and writing lines

Let's start by iterating over a collection and writing each value as a line to an output file:

```
const myList = Range()
  .map(v => `Value${v}`)
  .take(20)
  .toList();
const output = fs.createWriteStream(
  './output/05-writing-collection-data'
);

output.on('close', () => {
```

```
    console.log('done');
});

myList.forEach((v) => {
  output.write((v + os.EOL));
});

output.end();
```

The values that we're trying to write to a file are simple strings from `myList`. The output stream is ready for writing as soon as it's created with `fs.createWriteStream()`. In the side-effect we've created with `forEach()`, we're writing each value from the collection to the output stream using the `write()` method. When the `forEach()` loop exits, we signal that we're done with the stream by calling `end()`. The resulting file contents should look like this:

```
Value0
Value1
Value2
Value3
Value4
Value5
Value6
Value7
Value8
Value9
...
```

This technique works fine for smaller collections. Once you start working with larger collections, you could end up calling `write()` faster than data is actually written to the underlying stream resource.

Asynchronous data and sequences

Let's say that you have the following sequence that you need to write to a file:

```
const mySeq = Range(1)
  .filterNot(v => v % 10)
  .take(1000);
```

You want to be able to iterate over this sequence to produce a side-effect that writes each value as a line in a file. However, since this is a larger collection, you run the risk of running out of buffer space in the stream before it's flushed to the open file. This could cause errors in your application.

To cope with this situation, streams provide us with two tools. When we call `write()`, it will return `false` if the stream buffer is full. When the `drain` event fires, this indicates that the stream is ready to accept more `write()` calls. Let's create a utility function to handle this scenario for us:

```
const write = (stream, data) => new Promise((resolve) => {
  if (stream.write(data.toString() + os.EOL)) {
    resolve();
  } else {
    stream.once('drain', () => resolve());
  }
});
```

You can use this `write()` function by passing it a writable stream and the data that you want to write to it. The key idea of this function is that it returns a promise so that the calling code knows when the data has been written and can write more data. If `stream.write()` returns `true`, we resolve it right away. Otherwise, we have to wait for the `drain` event before we resolve the promise.

With this tool in place, we're ready to implement our side-effect:

```
const output = fs.createWriteStream(
  './output/06-writing-sequence-data'
);

output.on('close', () => {
  console.log('done');
});

mySeq.forEach(async (value) => {
  await write(output, value);
});

output.end();
```

We're passing `forEach()` an asynchronous function here. This allows us to use `await` to pause execution until `write()` resolves. Since `write()` doesn't resolve until it's safe to start writing more data, it's safe to use it in a loop like this.

Chaining lazy sequences and streams

You saw how to deal with asynchronous stream operations in the preceding example. In a typical Node.js application, input streams are joined together with output streams while data is transformed as it flows through the application. This fits quite well with all Immutable.js processing patterns. So let's take a stab at chaining together streams that lazily process collection data as more data is available to read, and more data is able to be written.

We'll start by creating an input stream that reads from the `words` file. We'll pipe it to other streams using the `pipe()` method:

```
const wordInput = fs.createReadStream('./input/words');

wordInput
  .pipe(seqTransform)
  .pipe(filterAndMapTransform)
  .pipe(myWritable);
```

We're essentially chaining together the actions of the three chains that `wordInput` has piped together. Let's start by looking at the `seqTransform` stream:

```
const seqTransform = new Transform({
  objectMode: true,
  transform(chunk, encoding, callback) {
    const last = this.last || '';
    const words = (last + chunk.toString()).split(os.EOL);

    this.last = words[words.length - 1];
    this.push(Seq(words));
    callback();
  }
});
```

A `Transform` stream has both an input and an output stream inside of it. These are set up when we call `pipe()`. We're using the same approach as we used earlier in the chapter, where we split the chunk of data into an array, making sure that the last word is saved for the next chunk. The `transform()` method that we've implemented here is called automatically as more input data becomes available.

When we're ready to write data to the output stream, we call `this.push()`. The idea of this particular transformation is to transform the current chunk into an Immutable.js sequence: `this.push(Seq(words))`.

Normally, streams communicate by passing buffers. If you want to pass around other objects such as Immutable.js collections, you have to enable `objectMode`.

Next, let's look at the `filterAndMapTransform` stream:

```
const filterAndMapTransform = new Transform({
  objectMode: true,
  transform(seq, encoding, callback) {
    seq
      .filter(v => v.length >= 15)
      .map(v => v.toUpperCase())
      .forEach(v => this.push(v));
    callback();
  }
});
```

Things are really starting to come together at this point. This stream gets a sequence collection passed to it from `seqTransform`. Then we can perform our `filter()` and `map()` calls, while each value is passed to the output stream as it flows through the sequence of operations.

The bottom line is this: as input data becomes available, we turn this into a sequence and lazily process values, passing them to the output stream one at a time while we wait for more input data.

Finally, let's look at the `myWritable` stream:

```
const myWritable = new Writable({
  write(chunk, encoding, callback) {
    console.log('writing', chunk.toString());
    callback();
  }
});
```

We didn't actually need to create `myWritable`. For example, if this were to be written to a file, we'd simply pipe it to an output stream with a file open for writing. However, we're trying to write specialized logs as the output. Here's what the console output looks like:

```
writing SEMISENTIMENTAL
writing SEMISERIOUSNESS
writing SEMISIGHTSEEING
writing SEMISOMNAMBULISTIC
writing SEMISOVEREIGNTY
writing SEMISPECULATION
...
```

Summary

In this chapter, you learned about Immutable.js collection side-effects in Node.js applications. We started by looking at how to read and parse input data into collection data. Then we looked at more efficient means to build large collections out of large amounts of input data.

Next, we looked at writing data from Immutable.js collections. First, you wrote simple output to files from small collections. Then, we addressed the asynchronous nature of writing larger amounts of data and how to build abstractions around this. We then chained together many streams and lazily-evaluated sequence data.

In the final chapter of this book, we'll tie up some loose ends, and put together a coherent Immutable.js architecture that you can use in more than just one application.

16
Immutable Architecture

The final chapter of this book is about putting together the tools and techniques that you've learned from previous chapters into a cohesive application architecture. You'll expand on the application that you built in `Chapter 14`, *Side-Effects in User Interfaces*, and by doing so, you'll learn about the following:

- Creating a generic application state updater component
- Providing initial state and side-effect functions
- Updating the application state in response to user events
- Running side-effects in response to state updates

The reusable application state updater

To create a sustainable architecture for your Immutable.js code, you need a component that handles a few things:

- It encapsulates the entire application state as one nested Immutable.js collection
- It provides a mechanism for changing the application state by passing in a new Immutable.js collection
- It runs side-effect functions every time the state changes

Such a component would be generic and useful enough so that you could use it in all of your Immutable.js applications. The idea is to enforce consistent side-effect behavior in response to state changes. Let's implement this component now.

Initial state

For lack of a better name, we'll call this component `App()`. In essence, it is the app since it holds all of the application state and all of the side-effects that control what the user sees. To start, we have to pass the component the initial state of our application. The initial state is used by side-effects to perform the initial render. Then, once the user starts interacting with the UI, we can change the initial state.

We could pass the initial state into the component like this:

```
App(Map.of(
  'first', '',
  'last', '',
  'age', 0
));
```

The application state, in this case, is represented by a map with three key-value pairs. The values are two empty strings and an `age` of zero, which probably isn't very meaningful to the user. It doesn't matter though, because the side-effect functions that rely on this state have something to render initially. Once we change any or all of these values, the side-effects will run again, rendering relevant information.

Immutable.js collections are good at reusing data when mutative methods are called. This is how you're able to use a single map as your application state. You'll probably want to organize the state of your application into sections that reflect the on-screen organization of your UI. This probably means creating nested collections in your application state:

```
App(Map.of(
  'home', Map.of(
    'showUpdates', true,
    'updates', List.of(
      'Update 1...',
      'Update 2...'
    )
  ),
  'users', Map.of(
    'visible', false,
    'users', Set()
  ),
  'settings', Map.of(
    'emailLevel', 'ultraspam',
    'resultsPerPage', 10
  )
));
```

With this initial state in place, your side-effects can run. This also gives you a sense of what's likely to change in response to user interactions. For example, if a new update gets pushed to the `updates` list in the `home` map, the rest of the application state remains unchanged. Also, this initial state helps form the shape of your side-effect functions.

Side-effects

The other thing we'll want to pass to the `App()` function are the side-effect functions. The aim is to pass the side-effect functions that handle one slice of the overall application state. There's little point in having a side-effect function that runs in response to every conceivable state change. In fact, we can map side-effect functions in the same way as we do with the state itself:

```
App(
  Map.of(
    'home', Map.of(...),
    'users', Map.of(...),
    'settings', Map.of(...)
  ),
  Map.of(
    'home', (home) => { ... },
    'users', (users) => { ... },
    'settings', (settings) => { ... }
  )
);
```

The map with the side-effect functions closely resembles the application state map. This allows us to run certain behavior when a certain part of the state changes. For example, if something in the `home` state changes, we want to run the side-effect that uses the `home` state as input. This allows us to split up our side-effect code into targeted functions that do one thing.

However, even just one part of the application state could represent a screen in our UI that has lots of moving parts. Trying to fit all of these updates into one side-effect function could be difficult. So, let's assume that `App()` needs to be able to handle running more than one side-effect function per state update. We could pass in the functions like this:

```
App(
  Map.of(
    'home', Map.of(...),
    'users', Map.of(...),
    'settings', Map.of(...)
  ),
  Map.of(
```

```
        'home', Seq.of(
          (home) => { console.log('home side-effect 1'); },
          (home) => { console.log('home side-effect 2'); }
        ),
        'users', Seq.of(
          (users) => { console.log('users side-effect 1'); },
          (users) => { console.log('users side-effect 2'); }
        ),
        'settings', Seq.of(
          (settings) => { console.log('settings side-effect 1'); },
          (settings) => { console.log('settings side-effect 2'); }
        )
      )
    );
```

With an `App()` function like this in place, we can see the data in our application and what happens when it changes. Now we just have to implement `App()` and have it return a function that will update the application state for us.

Updating state and running side-effects

Let's implement the basic concepts of the `App()` function, and then we'll circle back and fill in some details. The function takes a collection representing the initial state of the application and a collection representing the side-effect functions to run when the state changes. We need a tool that allows us to update this state now. Maybe we could return a function that accepts an `updater` function:

```
const App = (initialState, sideEffects) => {
  let state = initialState;

  return (updater) => {
    const newState = updater(state);
    state = newState;
  };
};
```

The `App()` function stores the `initialState` value in the `state` variable. This is where any changes in the `state` variable will be made. It also returns a new function that will be used for all future state updates. In a way, `App()` is like a class used in a singleton pattern. The resulting function is the singleton that's used throughout the application. We pass it a callback function that receives the application state as it's argument, and it returns the new application state. Let's look at how you would go about using the global state updater function returned by `App()`:

```
const app = App(
  Map.of(...), // Initial state...
  Map.of(...)  // Side-effect functions...
);

app(state => state.set('foo', 'bar'));
```

As you can see, the `app()` function that we've created here is important and needs to be accessible throughout the application. Whenever we need to change the application state, we use this function. In this example, we provide `app()` with a callback function that calls `set()` on the `state` argument and returns a new map. This is how the new state is set. The last thing to implement is running the side-effect functions in response to state changes:

```
const App = (initialState, sideEffects) => {
  let state = initialState;
  state.forEach((v, k) => {
    List()
      .concat(sideEffects.get(k))
      .forEach(sideEffect => sideEffect(v));
  });

  return (updater) => {
    const newState = updater(state);

    newState.forEach((v, k) => {
      if (v !== state.get(k)) {
        List()
          .concat(sideEffects.get(k))
          .forEach(sideEffect => sideEffect(v));
      }
    });

    state = newState;
  };
};
```

The first `forEach()` loop is used to perform the initial side-effect function calls against the initial state. The second `forEach()` loop is used to perform side-effects when the state changes. Note that we're checking to see if the state has actually changed (`v !== state.get(k)`) before running the side-effects for the given piece of state. If the state hasn't changed for a given piece of state, we know that the UI currently reflects the piece of state as it is.

With these 20 lines of code, we now have a reusable component that serves as the architectural driver for our Immutable.js applications. Now let's work on building our Black Mirror application from `Chapter 14`, *Side-Effects in User Interfaces*, using this new architecture.

Initial application state

We'll start refactoring our application by thinking about the initial state of it. This will help us figure out how to break the whole state down into parts that can be mutated individually. We'll also add a new feature to this version of the app that allows the user to add new episodes. Here's what this part of the UI looks like:

Another new feature that we'll add to this version of the app is displaying the number of results beside the header:

As the filter controls change, and as new episodes are added, this number will change. Apart from these two changes, the functionality stays the same.

Result state

The first piece of state that we'll look at is the episode search results. This is the focal point of the application, so this is where we'll see the most action. For example, it would make sense to store the list of all episodes here. Also, we'll want to keep track of the states of the various filter controls here:

```
const app = App(
  Map.of(
    'results', Map.of(
      'episodes', List.of(
        Map.of(
          'title', 'The National Anthem',
          'date', 'December 4 2011',
          'director', 'Otto Bathurst',
          'rating', 8.0
        ),
        ...
      ),
      'query', '',
      'title', true,
      'director', false,
      'date', false,
      'rating', 7
    ),
  )
);
```

Inside the `results` state, we have the list of episodes. We also have the filter control states. The `query` state is an empty string initially, because the user isn't looking for something the first time the page is rendered. The `title` state is true initially because we want this checkbox selected by default. The initial `rating` state is 7, which should be reflected visually by the rating slider.

Creating a new episode state

The only other piece of state that we need to consider for this UI is the new **Create Episode** form. Just as we track the state of the filter controls in the results state, we need to track the state of new data as it's entered so that we have it when the user clicks on the **Create** button:

```
const app = App(Map.of(
  'results', Map.of(...),
  'create', Map.of(
    'title', '',
```

```
      'director', '',
      'date', '',
      'rating', 0
   )
);
```

In the previous implementation of this example, we just looked up the values that we needed directly from the form elements. There's nothing wrong with doing this, but since we're trying to keep our application state all together in one place, it would be confusing to look up some state in our App component and other state directly from DOM elements.

Events and state updaters

We have our initial application state, and we have our app() function that's used to produce new state. Now we have to figure out the various ways in which our application state mutates in response to user interactions.

Updating the search query

As the user types, we want to render only episodes that match the search text. To do this, we have to use our app() function to update the state. Here's what this looks like:

```
document
  .querySelector('header input[type="search"]')
  .addEventListener('input', e => app(state => state.setIn(
    ['results', 'query'],
    e.target.value
  )));
```

The setIn() function is used here to set the query state, nested inside of the results state. The array that's passed to setIn() is a path to follow as the map is traversed. The value is updated to reflect the value of the search input box.

Realizing that all we're doing here is changing the state of the application is important. We're not actually running the filter—this is part of the side-effect that uses the results state.

Updating the checkboxes and slider state

The episode results should also be updated in response to the checkboxes and rating slider being changed. Here's what these handlers look like:

```
document
  .querySelector('li input[name="title"]')
  .addEventListener('change', e => app(state => state.setIn(
    ['results', 'title'],
    e.target.checked
  )));
document
  .querySelector('li input[name="director"]')
  .addEventListener('change', e => app(state => state.setIn(
    ['results', 'director'],
    e.target.checked
  )));
document
  .querySelector('li input[name="date"]')
  .addEventListener('change', e => app(state => state.setIn(
    ['results', 'date'],
    e.target.checked
  )));
document
  .getElementById('filter-rating')
  .addEventListener('change', e => app(state => state.setIn(
    ['results', 'rating'],
    e.target.value
  )));
```

The job of event handlers is to update the application state and nothing more.

Updating new episode data

As the user enters new data into the **Create Episode** form, we have to update the create state. This works much in the same way as the form controls that filter episodes:

```
document
  .querySelector('form[name="create-episode"] input[name="title"]')
  .addEventListener('input', e => app(state => state.setIn(
    ['create', 'title'],
    e.target.value
  )));
document
  .querySelector('form[name="create-episode"] input[name="director"]')
  .addEventListener('input', e => app(state => state.setIn(
```

```
      ['create', 'director'],
      e.target.value
    )));
document
  .querySelector('form[name="create-episode"] input[name="date"]')
  .addEventListener('input', e => app(state => state.setIn(
    ['create', 'date'],
    e.target.value
  )));
document
  .getElementById('new-episode-rating')
  .addEventListener('change', e => app(state => state.setIn(
    ['create', 'rating'],
    e.target.value
  )));
```

When these state values are updated, nothing in the UI changes. This is because we're not actually using these values for anything until the user clicks on the **Create** button.

Creating new episodes

When we create a new episode and add it to the list of episode maps, we're actually updating two pieces of state. We're updating the `results` state because this is where the episodes list is located. We're also updating the `create` state to reset the form field values back to empty strings:

```
document
  .querySelector('form[name="create-episode"]')
  .addEventListener('submit', (e) => {
    e.preventDefault();
    app(state => state
      .updateIn(
        ['results', 'episodes'],
        episodes => episodes.push(
          Map(state.get('create').toJS())
        )
      )
      .setIn(['create', 'title'], '')
      .setIn(['create', 'director'], '')
      .setIn(['create', 'date'], '')
    );
  });
```

Here we're chaining together several mutative methods that change the state of the application. First, we're adding the new episode based on the current `create` state. Then we can reset the `create` state so that the new episode values are removed from the form. As a result, the user sees an updated form and the new episode in the results list, assuming that it meets the current filter criteria.

Executing side-effects

So far, we have an application that provides the initial state and then updates this state in response to user interactions. The final thing we need to build are the actual side-effect functions that execute in response to changing the state.

Rendering episode results

Any piece of state within the `results` state has the potential to change what's rendered on the screen. If an episode is added, removed, or changed, the list needs to be rendered. If a filter control changes, the list needs to be rendered because the current list might not reflect the current filter settings.

We'll still use the same filtering approach used in `Chapter 14`, *Side-Effects in User Interfaces*, though with a few minor adjustments:

```
const filter = ({
  query,
  title,
  date,
  director,
  rating
}) => every(
  some(
    () => query === undefined,
    () => query === '',
    every(
      () => title,
      v => v.get('title').includes(query)
    ),
    every(
      () => date,
      v => v.get('date').includes(query)
    ),
    every(
      () => director,
```

```
        v => v.get('director').includes(query)
      )
    ),
    v => v.get('rating') >= (+rating)
  );
```

The main difference is in how the values are passed into the function as arguments. This changed because we can no longer rely on global data from DOM nodes. Then we have the actual side-effect function:

```
const app = App(
  Map.of(...),
  Map.of(
    'results', Seq.of(
      (results) => {
        removeChildren(
          document
            .getElementById('results')
            .querySelector('ul')
        );

        results
          .get('episodes')
          .toSeq()
          .filter(filter(results.toJS()))
          .forEach((v) => {
            const { content } = document
              .getElementById('episode-template');

            content
              .querySelector('h4')
              .textContent = v.get('title');
            content
              .querySelector('p:nth-of-type(1)')
              .childNodes[1]
              .nodeValue = v.get('date');
            content
              .querySelector('p:nth-of-type(2)')
              .childNodes[1]
              .nodeValue = v.get('director');
            content
              .querySelector('p:nth-of-type(3)')
              .childNodes[1]
              .nodeValue = v.get('rating');

            document
              .getElementById('results')
              .querySelector('ul')
```

```
      .appendChild(document.importNode(content, true));
    });
  }
 )
 )
);
```

Just like we did in `Chapter 14`, *Side-Effects in User Interfaces*, we filter the list of episodes and render them. This time, we don't have to call this function manually, because it's passed to `App()` as a side-effect, set to run whenever the results state changes.

Rendering the result count

Let's add a separate side-effect function that updates the result count:

```
const app = App(Map.of(
  Map.of(...),
  Map.of(
    'results', Seq.of(
      (results) => {
        const count = results
          .get('episodes')
          .toSeq()
          .filter(filter(results.toJS()))
          .count();

        document
          .getElementById('results')
          .querySelector('h3')
          .textContent = document
          .getElementById('results')
          .querySelector('h3')
          .textContent
          .replace(/\d*/, count);
      },
    )
  )
));
```

In this case, we're executing the same query that's executed when the episodes are rendered, except in this function, we're counting values instead of iterating over the results. On the one hand, we have a separate side-effect function to handle rendering the result count. On the other hand, we're being inefficient with our filters by executing them more than once. Luckily, we can easily refactor our side-effect functions to combine multiple side-effect functions into one.

Resetting the new episode form

The last side-effect for us to implement is for the **Create New Episode** form data:

```
const app = App(Map.of(
  Map.of(...),
  Map.of(
    'results', Map.of(...),
    'create', Seq.of(
      (create) => {
        document
          .getElementById('new-episode-rating')
          .value = create.get('rating');
        document
          .querySelector('form[name="create-episode"] input[name="title"]')
          .value = create.get('title');
        document
          .querySelector('form[name="create-episode"]
input[name="director"]')
          .value = create.get('director');
        document
          .querySelector('form[name="create-episode"] input[name="date"]')
          .value = create.get('date');
        document
          .querySelector('output[for="new-episode-rating"]')
          .value = create.get('rating');
      }
    )
  )
);
```

This is a simple side-effect, all it needs to do is to update the form field values. This happens when the user clicks on the **Create** button and we want the form fields to empty.

Summary

In this chapter, you learned how to design and implement an architecture for your Immutable.js abstraction. We started by building a reusable component that takes the initial application state and side-effect functions as arguments and returns an updater function, which is then used throughout the application to update the application state. This component runs the appropriate side-effect whenever state changes.

Then you implemented another version of the application from Chapter 14, *Side-Effects in User Interfaces*, where we listed Black Mirror episodes. This implementation used our new App() component to encapsulate immutable state and to orchestrate the execution of our side-effect functions.

I hope this has been an enlightening read. I set out to write this book with the hope of sharing some of my hard-earned knowledge working with Immutable.js in production for many years. With the skills you've picked up in this book, I'm confident that you'll be able to tackle any problem that comes your way by wielding Immutable.js collection awesomeness.

Index

www.ingramcontent.com/pod-product-compliance
Lightning Source LLC
Chambersburg PA
CBHW080526060326
40690CB00022B/5035